The Well-Appointed Bath

AUTHENTIC PLANS AND FIXTURES FROM THE EARLY 1900s

....

INTRODUCTION BY GAIL CASKEY WINKLER

CHARLES E. FISHER III, GENERAL EDITOR

Landmark Reprint Series

THE PRESERVATION PRESS

NATIONAL TRUST FOR HISTORIC PRESERVATION

The Preservation Press
National Trust for Historic Preservation
1785 Massachusetts Avenue, N.W.
Washington, D.C. 20036

The National Trust for Historic Preservation is the only private, national non-profit organization chartered by Congress to encourage public participation in the preservation of sites, buildings and objects significant in American history and culture. Support is provided by membership dues, endowment funds, contributions and grants from federal agencies, including the U.S. Department of the Interior, under provisions of the National Historic Preservation Act of 1966. The opinions expressed here do not necessarily reflect the opinions or policies of the Interior Department. For information about membership, write to the Membership Department at the address above.

Printed in the United States of America
95 94 93 92 91 90 89 5 4 3 2 1

Library of Congress Cataloging in Publication Data

The Well-appointed bath : authentic plans and fixtures from the early 1900s /
   introduction by Gail Caskey Winkler ; Charles E. Fisher, general editor
      p.   cm.   — (Landmark reprint series)
   Includes reproduction of two bathroom fixture catalogs from 1914 and
c. 1935 published respectively by Mott and Standard.
   ISBN 0-89133-151-4
   1. Plumbing fixtures — Catalogs. 2. Bathrooms — Designs and plans —
Catalogs. I. Winkler, Gail Caskey. II. Fisher, Charles E. (Charles Elbert),
1947–   . III. Series.
TH6255.W44 1989
696'.1'029473 — dc 19   89-3613

Modern Plumbing, Number 8, is reproduced courtesy Smithsonian Institution Libraries Collections. This publication shall not be reproduced in whole or in part without prior written permission of the Smithsonian Institution Libraries.

Planning Your Plumbing Wisely is reproduced courtesy The Athenaeum of Phildelphia.

The Preservation Press gratefully acknowledges the assistance of American Standard in the publication of this book.

Edited by Diane Maddex, director, and Janet Walker, managing editor,
The Preservation Press
Designed by Anne Masters, Washington, D.C.
Composed in Goudy Oldstyle by General Typographers, Washington, D.C.
Color separations by Dodge Color, Washington, D.C.
Printed by the John D. Lucas Printing Company, Baltimore, Md.

Contents

Acknowledgments

The Preservation Press is grateful to American Standard for its support of this book made possible through the efforts of Michael Suzanski, marketing director, and John Laughton, manager of marketing projects, U.S. Plumbing Products Division.

The National Park Service, American Society of Interior Designers and other sponsors of the 1988 Interiors Conference for Historic Buildings were instrumental in identifying the importance of using historic trade catalogs in the rehabilitation of historic buildings. This book was initiated at the suggestion of Charles E. Fisher III of the National Park Service, who provided invaluable advice and assistance throughout its publication.

Charles Fisher wishes to thank the following individuals who assisted with this effort: Jim Roan, librarian, National Museum of American History, Smithsonian Institution; Nancy L. Matthews, publications officer, Smithsonian Institution Libraries; Roger W. Moss, executive director, and Bruce Laverty, archivist, The Athenaeum of Philadelphia; Rebecca Shiffer, architectural historian, National Park Service; and members of the planning committe for the 1988 Interiors Conference, particularly Tom Keohan, National Park Service; Larry Jones, Robert Meadows Architects; Michael Lynch, New York State Office of Parks, Recreation and Historic Preservation; and Chuck Parrott, Lowell Historic Preservation Commission. Special thanks go to the Historic Preservation Education Foundation for providing early funding assistance to research historic trade catalogs.

Gail Caskey Winkler wishes to thank the following persons for their assistance with the introduction: Susan Finkel, New Jersey State Museum, Trenton; Robert Lupp and Rebecca Colesar, New Jersey State Library, Trenton; Willard Marrion, American Standard, Piscataway, N.J.; William E. Massey, Jr., Crane Plumbing, Atlanta; Richard W. Reeves, Free Public Library, Trenton; Rodris Roth, Smithsonian Institution, Washington, D.C.; and Leah Weisse, Kohler Company, Kohler, Wis. Much of the author's research was conducted at The Athenaeum of Philadelphia, which has an excellent collection of plumbing trade catalogs. She particularly appreciates the assistance of Keith A. Kamm, bibliographer; Jane Reiter, assistant bibliographer; and Louis Meehan, photographer. All illustrations in the introduction are reproduced with permission from The Athenaeum of Philadelphia collection.

Foreword

JOHN W. CLARKE

Vice President

American Standard

I was delighted to learn that the National Trust for Historic Preservation was publishing this book.

At American Standard, our sights are on a future in which bathrooms of increasing elegance, quality and practicality are enjoyed by a growing number of people, both in our country and throughout the world. Certainly, with manufacturing units in so many countries abroad, we are helping raise standards for people internationally.

However, we will undoubtedly plan a better future if we appreciate and value the achievements of our predecessors in the industry. This nation — and my company in particular — has been a prime mover in making fine bathrooms available to a widening section of the population over the last century, with all that this has brought in pleasure, comfort and hygiene. The history of bathing is a long one, stretching back to such early civilizations as Minoa and ancient Rome. But the modern bathroom, with its potential availability to all people, began its phenomenal growth in the United States and spread from here to other parts of the industrialized world and then to the world at large.

As this book so clearly shows, all in today's plumbing products industry — manufacturers, distributors, contractors and designers — are heirs to a fine tradition. And the promises of the future that are the focus of our attention today are rooted in an illustrious past.

Preface

CHARLES E. FISHER III

With the publication of *The Well-Appointed Bath*, we hope to introduce a series of reprints of late 19th- and early 20th-century manufacturers' trade catalogs for building products and furnishings. Published by many firms after the Civil War, illustrated catalogs quickly became an accepted means of publicizing and marketing products in this competitive era. Today, these old catalogs have become valuable resources for documenting the architecture of the last hundred years.

As windows to the past, the period trade catalogs are also proving their usefulness as practical guides for restoring and rehabilitating historic buildings. They can help document surviving features, fixtures and furnishings in a building; guide development of restoration plans; and aid the selection of appropriate reproduction material or traditional finishes. They even provide an understanding of period construction and installation details that can save time and help avoid damage to historic features during rehabilitation. But trade catalogs, historic or contemporary, should always be used with some caution. No manufacturers' literature can ever be relied on exclusively to make preservation decisions.

The Well-Appointed Bath reprints two catalogs of bathroom fixtures from the early 20th century: the 1914 *Modern Plumbing* catalog (Number 8) by the J. L. Mott Iron Works of New York and *Planning Your Plumbing Wisely,* published in the mid-1930s by the Standard Sanitary Manufacturing Company of Pittsburgh (later American Standard). Predictably, the bathroom — more than any other room of the American home — has been the least understood and appreciated in its contribution to the design and history of our everyday environment. Only since the early 1980s have architects and designers routinely treated the bathroom with a seriousness equal to other principal living areas of the American home. Yet, as manufacturers, both the J. L. Mott and Standard Sanitary companies challenged the architect, builder and homeowner of their time to thoughtfully design and purchase fixtures that would make the bathroom cheerful, comfortable and elegant. Whether in new construction or remodeling, both manufacturers described numerous ways to design and select a well-appointed bath, including schemes that were sensitive to a homeowner's modest budget.

Little has been written on the evolution of the modern bathroom that would be of much help to individuals rehabilitating or restoring early 20th-century homes. This is remarkable in that the bathroom, as an integral part of the American home, is a product of the last hundred years. As Gail Caskey Winkler indicates in her introduction, bathrooms emerged as a commonplace feature as a result of post–Civil War industrialization, of improved sanitation in both the home and urban areas, and, ultimately, of the convenience they represented.

The recent facsimile reprint of the J. L. Mott Iron Works Catalog G, originally published in 1888, serves as an excellent reminder of the rapid pace and significant change that occurred in bathroom design and fixtures when compared to the 1914 Mott catalog here. The essential components of the modern bathroom had, for the most part, been established by 1914. With popularization in the mid-1930s of the built-in or recessed combination bath and shower — displayed in the Standard brochure — the modern bathroom was largely defined. Some observations follow on these two important publications and how they can be used.

MODERN PLUMBING
Mott's 1914 *Modern Plumbing* catalog, reproduced here in its entirety at a slight reduction, includes 26 bathroom plans and more than 200 illustrations of bathroom products. While some exhibit Victorian traits, others, such as the "Noveau" plan, were quite modern.

The plans are particularly instructive, showing the selection and placement of fixtures and accessories as well as lighting and wall and floor designs. And, just like today, the plans had an advertising goal — to influence and direct the buyer to purchase the more expensive items and, moreover, to buy the complete "package" offered by Mott. Many display an extensive use of wall and floor tiles, a product and installation service offered by Mott that would become commonplace by the 1930s.

The catalog contains a wealth of practical information and design guidance, such as using oval-shaped mirrors over oval sinks and rectangular mirrors over rectangular sinks. Nickel plating is shown as the standard finish for brass faucets and accessory items such as towel racks. A standard practice for manufacturers in this era, Mott supplied fixtures complete with fittings and faucets and, in the case of showers, even the curtain rod, hooks and the curtain itself! Prices of individual room plans typically included the bath, shower (if featured), water closet (toilet with seat) and lavatory (sink). Mirrors, medicine cabinets and other furnishings were extra. The state-of-the-art white celluloid-enamel finish on toilet seats was quoted as a standard item but was actually top-of-the-line for its time, and thus considerably more expensive than the traditional varnished wood seats.

The fully recessed bath was still not common during this era, and only one Mott design, the expensive "Prescott" plan, incorporated a recessed bath and shower combination. The sanitary and housekeeping advantages of hiding pipes in the wall and recessing the bath eventually outweighed the additional expense of installation to become standard features of modern bathrooms.

The Mott trademark was familiar in its time and is often found on surviving fixtures. Perhaps with the benefit of this reprint, there will be a rediscovery of Mott products still in use in old homes and a heightened interest in preserving rather than replacing these traditional American features.

PLANNING YOUR PLUMBING WISELY
The vibrant colors in the facsimile reprint from the Standard Sanitary Manufacturing Company, published in the mid-1930s, attest to a revolution in bathroom design that resulted from the introduction of colored fixtures. Even toilet seats were available in colors. This break from the sanitized white bathroom of previous decades encouraged creativity in room plans as well. The recessed bath and shower combination was now an accepted practice. New designs included recesses for the sink and "hidden" water closets, niches for towels and built-in medicine cabinets. Colored wall tiles and decoratively patterned linoleum, fanciful shower curtains, metal trim and more extensive use of mirrors added to the exciting new look.

Besides small design changes in fixtures, such as cut-off corners in the

"Hexagon" lavatory, the Standard trademark could be found on bold new designs, such as the "Neo-Angle" bath, where emphasis was on comfort, convenience and safety. Chrome-plated brass fittings were being marketed in lieu of nickel plate, offering a tarnish-free finish. Yet some of the products promoted, including the single hot and cold water faucets for lavatories, were not as new as the advertising suggests. Mott had offered numerous such faucets 20 years earlier.

Several plans that show the before-and-after look are not only interesting historically, they also reveal Standard's marketing approach — keeping an eye to remodeling as well as new construction. While Mott promoted the advantages of the second bathroom, Standard stressed the convenience of the additional half-bath, a feature that became quite common in the American home. Although still in the midst of the Depression, Standard proudly noted that financing was available for remodeling. Other practical advice included the warning that "cleaning powders should be selected with care as gritty cleansers will affect any glossy surface" — excellent preservation advice even today for discerning homeowners.

The Mott and Standard catalogs share certain qualities that make them particularly worthy of reprinting. Both companies were large manufacturers of their day, with offices and showrooms in major cities across the United States. American Standard, a widely recognized name, is a giant today in plumbing fixtures. Mott was less fortunate, however, going out of business during the Depression. Both publications go well beyond a routine cataloging of available fixtures. Featuring room layouts — complete with fixtures, furnishings and wall finishes — they deal with the total bathroom and provide us with excellent illustrations of the one room in the home that was rarely photographed. While portions of each catalog describe traditional items (including some that were *retardataire* in their day), each also proudly displays its newest lines. Their narratives provide further insight into the social influences, health considerations and economic facts that affected the evolution of this most private of rooms. Finally, both catalogs help open the door to our least studied room, expanding our appreciation of the history of the bathroom in the American home and, as a result, assisting today's preservation efforts.

Introduction

GAIL CASKEY WINKLER

The two early 20th-century catalogs reprinted in this book illustrate fixtures that are surprisingly modern in appearance. Here, more than 50 years ago, are pedestal sinks, enameled double-shell tubs, siphonic-jet toilets — all looking much like their present counterparts — along with the colored porcelains, ceramic tiles and marble finishes that are still considered the hallmarks of the well-appointed bath. The "toilet tables" with dainty hand basins pictured in the 1914 catalog of the J. L. Mott Iron Works are no longer produced, but the other fixtures, including bidets, sold by Mott and the Standard Sanitary Manufacturing Company (today, American Standard) have come to us virtually unchanged since the first decades of the 20th century.

America was then the best-plumbed nation in the world. By 1940, 93.5 percent of all urban dwellings had running water, 83 percent had indoor toilets and 77.5 percent had bathing facilities. As described in the following pages, such advances were the combined result of sanitarians' demands for improved municipal water and sewerage systems as well as manufacturing techniques perfected by companies such as Mott and Standard. These gains were not equally distributed, however. More than 40 percent of Americans lived in rural areas, where only 17.8 percent of the houses had running water and 11.2 percent were equipped with toilets and bathtubs.[1]

THE PHILOSOPHY OF CLEANLINESS
Although bathroom fixtures such as the ones presented in the Mott and Standard catalogs have changed little to the present, they were preceded by centuries of experimentation to achieve acceptable sanitation. In fact, the ancient world practiced better hygiene than did

most Americans and Europeans until the second half of the 19th century. The Minoan palace of Knossos was outfitted with bathtubs and running water 1,600 years B.C., and in the Greek Peloponnese, public toilets carved in stone have been excavated near the gates of the ancient city of Corinth. Every Roman city had its baths, the remains of which have been found as far north as England, where hot mineral waters still flow at Aquae Sulis (Bath). Yet more than 1,500 years later, in 1831, an anonymous writer in Godey's *Lady's Book* exclaimed, "The generality of English ladies seem to be ignorant of the use of any bath larger than a wash-hand basin."[2]

Their American cousins were no more enlightened. Harriet Martineau recorded in *Society in America* (1837): "In private houses, baths are a rarity. In steam-boats, the accommodations for washing are limited in the extreme; and in all but first-rate hotels, the philosophy of personal cleanliness is certainly not understood."[3] Improvised bathing facilities sometimes produced happy results. Fanny Kemble, the English actress who married a southern planter, praised the tubs made of cedar wood on their Georgia rice plantation in 1839. "The fragrance of these when they are first made, as well as their ample size, renders them preferable as dressing-room furniture, in my opinion, to all the china foot tubs that ever came out of Staffordshire."[4]

Those who argued that bathing was important for health and personal "daintiness" faced stiff opposition during the first decades of the 19th century.[5] Unheated rooms and tepid water offered little encouragement, yet Eliza Rotch Farrar felt compelled to devote nearly a chapter to bathing in her wildly popular etiquette book, *The Young Lady's Friend*, first published in 1837. She instructed her readers that "once, at least, in twenty-four hours, the whole surface of the body should be washed in soap and water, and receive the friction of a coarse towel, or flesh-brush, or crash [knitted, nubby cotton] mitten." With a bluntness generally not associated with Victorian culture, readers were told that "no one can be quite certain of never offending any one's delicate olfactory nerves, whose arm-pits are not subjected to a thorough washing with soap and water every day." Farrar would brook no excuse, not even cold rooms and limited facilities. "By washing a small part of the person at a time, rubbing it well, and then covering up what is done, the whole may be washed in cold water, even in winter time, and a glow may be produced after it, in a young and healthy person," she told her readers.[6] If their accommodations lacked the privacy of a dressing room, they were to rise before the rest of the household or retire later in order to bathe. "The whole surface of your body may be gone over with one large wash-bowl full of water," she told them, "and by practice you will become so expert as not to make any slop on the carpet. . . ."[7] Sponges — not washcloths — were used throughout the 19th century, and according to Godey's *Lady's Book*, a coarse "honey-comb" sponge held the most water and could actually substitute for a shower bath.[8]

Writers such as Martineau, Kemble and Farrar were voicing sentiments not shared by all segments of society. Urbane and sophisticated members of society were far more likely to bathe, apparently, than their country cousins. Farrar disparaged "the primitive manners of our fore-fathers (and of the back country at the present day), which required that every one should wash at the pump in the yard, or at the sink in the kitchen. . . ." Such habits, she concluded, "were not favorable to cleanliness and health."[9] Frederick Law Olmsted, the designer of Central Park, recounted an exchange between two American legislators from "the rural districts." In a subtle attempt to influence the appearance of his

acquaintance, one admitted that he changed his linen every day, to which his friend responded: "Why, what an awful dirty man you must be! I can always make mine last a week."[10] While this story is probably apocryphal, Olmsted's account of his travels along the lower Mississippi in 1857 described actual conditions. In one hotel room (which he was forced to share with a stranger), he found that "one wash-bowl, and a towel which had already been used, was expected to answer for both of us, and would have done so, but that I carried a private towel in my saddle-bags." Other plumbing, he added, was "unavailable with decency."[11]

ROOMS FOR THE MILLIONS — OR THE FEW?

American architects had begun to include bathrooms and water closets in the plans of "better" houses by the middle of the 19th century. In Andrew Jackson Downing's *The Architecture of Country Houses* (1850), eight of 13 villas — estimated to cost $4,600 to $14,000 — had water closets and bathrooms, but only one of the 13 cottage designs — costing between $400 and $3,000 — was so equipped. The lone exception was the cottage priced at $3,000. Downing noted that the presence of a water closet gave the "cottage quite a villa-like complete-

A copper bathtub in a simple wooden case. From the catalog of Hayden, Gere and Company of New York and Haydenville, Mass., 1866. (All illustrations from The Athenaeum of Philadelphia)

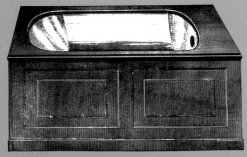

A sheet-metal tub in a more ornate boxing. From the Hayden, Gere and Company catalog, 1877.

ness."[12] Other architects showed similar restrictions. William H. Ranlett stated that his designs published in *The Architect* (1849) were "intended for the million as for the wealthy few," yet a bathroom and water closet appeared in only one house costing less than $3,500. Henry Hudson Holly included plumbing amenities in most of his 28 designs illustrated in *Country Seats* (1863); however, all but three were estimated at $3,000 or more.

As these architectural pattern books suggest, prosperous families living in rural or suburban areas at mid-century often had more amenities than their urban counterparts. Primitive water delivery systems had been completed in only a few American cities — such as Philadelphia in 1801 and New York in 1842 — and the vast majority of American homes were not piped for water. When the Philadelphia architect John Notman designed a home for Charles L. Pearson on the outskirts of Trenton, N.J., in 1849, he placed a thousand-gallon reservoir in the third story of the tower above the bath and water closet. The lead-lined reservoir held spring water supplied by a hydraulic ram pump.[13] Downing described such a system in 1850:

> Most of the new villas lately erected are supplied with water (through a tank in the roof) by that most perfect and simple of all little machines — the Hydraulic ram. By the aid of this, a small stream or overflowing spring, within 1000 feet of the site of the house, may be made to supply all the bed-rooms, water closets, and kitchen offices with water.[14]

In Search of Warmth

Hot water was an even greater luxury. While Godey's *Lady's Book*, the most widely read 19th-century magazine for women, echoed Eliza Farrar's sentiments that bathing in cold water built strength and that one accustomed to it would rarely feel temperature fluctuations during the winter months, a dependable supply of hot water and central heating were undoubtedly more enticing. Notman's heating system for the Pearson home kept the entire house at 70 degrees throughout the winter.[15] Louis Godey, publisher of the *Lady's Book*, praised the hot-air furnaces and kitchen ranges of Benjamin M. Feltwell, brick mason and stove manufacturer — and informed his readers that he had three in his Philadelphia home — because they could guarantee a warm bath at any time of day.[16] In a diary entry of December 20, 1852, prosperous and snobbish Sidney George Fisher described the bathroom in his Philadelphia house:

A paneled tub surround and backsplash. From the J. L. Mott Iron Works catalog, 1881.

My habits now are to rise at 7. I go to my dressing room which is in the back building & is very comfortable, having a bath with hot & cold water & a water closet adjoining, also a sink to carry off waste water & slops, all which are among the modern improvements which add so much to the comfort of life & which are now contained in houses of moderate cost. The dressing room has no fire, which I prefer & shall have it so, unless the weather is very cold. I strip, use the flesh brush & go thro some exercises, sparring with an imaginary foe for about 10 minutes, which is a fine air bath & bracing excitement. I take not a cold bath, which is too severe, but make the water from 60 to 65, about the temperature that it is in the summer or early autumn. It is a great luxury . . . and is far preferable to my old fashion of a sponging bath which I used because I had no other in the old house.[17]

Fisher's belief in the widespread use of bathrooms — even in houses of "moderate cost" — was overly optimistic. According to Godey's *Lady's Book*, a majority of Philadelphia houses contained bathrooms only by 1876, and the magazine was probably correct. While Philadelphians had long enjoyed the reputation of being the cleanest Americans, only 3,521 baths were distributed among a population of nearly 340,000 in 1849. New York, in contrast, had only 1,361 baths for its population of 629,904 in 1855.[18]

THE PROBLEM OF SEWERAGE

Delivering clean water was a fairly easy problem to solve; the earliest systems using hollow logs had been replaced by cast-iron pipes in eastern cities during the first decades of the 19th century. From the street mains, smaller pipes of lead or tinned iron carried water to individual residences. Running water eliminated the burdens of carrying buckets of fresh water, removing slop jars and emptying chamber pots. Not surprisingly, the easy availability of running water quickly increased the demand for it and overtaxed a totally unprepared sewerage system. From the house, waste pipes ran to a backyard cesspool that required periodic emptying. This practice was little better than the primitive privy pits that Benjamin Franklin had condemned a century earlier as "magazines of putrefaction." Sewerage systems, most begun in the decades following the Civil War, were often laid in a piecemeal fashion so that the sewage from one neighborhood might contaminate the water supply in another. The increasing size of urban

A valve water closet, whose design suggests why mechanical toilets were enclosed in boxlike cases. From the Hayden, Gere and Company catalog, 1866.

A case for a water closet that could be ordered in mahogany or black walnut. From the Hayden, Gere and Company catalog, 1877.

A graphic example of the problems associated with backyard privies and water pumps. From Lawler's American Sanitary Plumbing *by James J. Lawler, 1896. (Dornsife Collection of The Victorian Society in America)*

populations and recurring epidemics of cholera and typhoid spurred the "sanitarian" movement that finally achieved success with the general acceptance of Louis Pasteur's "germ theory" of disease by the end of the 19th century. Only then were integrated sewerage systems and filtered, chlorinated water adopted in most major American cities.[19]

THE MID-CENTURY BATHROOM

As these challenges were met and gradually overcome, portable bathing and toilet facilities gave way to permanent installations. The variety of tubs — hip, sitz, plunge, slipper and douche — developed during the 18th and early 19th centuries were all made of sheet metal including planished copper or sheet iron coated with tin or zinc and painted. Frequently the interior was painted white or marbleized while the exterior was brown. Many of these tubs were quite small — and with good reason; they were filled and emptied by hand. Hot and cold running water eliminated these burdensome tasks, with the consequence that stationary bathtubs took the generous form of the plunge or lounge tub so familiar in American homes today. Still made of sheet metal, these tubs were encased in wood wainscoting to match the surrounding walls. Early wash basins and water closets were similarly framed in wood, and most were made of sheet metal as well.

Through the middle decades of the 19th century, the "pan" toilet was the

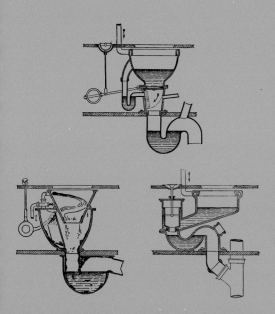

Cross sections of the three earliest types of toilets used in America: the pan, the valve and the plunger. From Hints on the Drainage and Sewerage of Dwellings by William Paul Gerhard, 1884.

An early cast-iron bathtub made by the J. L. Mott Iron Works. From the Hayden, Gere and Company catalog, 1866.

most common type used in America. The sloping sides of the basin and the movable pan at the bottom, both of sheet metal usually painted white, and the surrounding hopper of cast iron proved nearly impossible to flush clean. About 1865, valve and plunger closets began to replace the pan. Water was held in the basin, also made of sheet metal in the earliest models, by means of a valve or plunger leading to the trap and the soil pipe. After repeated use, the valve or plunger would cease to form a tight seal, resulting in water loss, incomplete flushes and odors. Lewis F. Allen hinted at these problems in *Rural Architecture* (1854):

> *A fashion prevails of thrusting these noisome things into the midst of sleeping chambers and living rooms — pandering to effeminacy, and, at times, surcharging the house — for they cannot, at all times, and under all circumstances, be kept perfectly close — with their offensive odor. Out of the house they belong; and if they, by any means, find their way within its walls proper, the fault will not be laid at our door.*[20]

Allen's designs isolated water closets in a ground-floor extension separated from the rest of the house. Most architects offered less extreme solutions and merely placed bathrooms and water closets at the back of the house — next to the servant's room. Despite these drawbacks, Catharine Beecher and Harriet Beecher Stowe undoubtedly echoed the sentiments of most women when they wrote in *The American Woman's Home* (1869): "Water-closets . . . cost no more than an out-door building, and save from the most disagreeable house-labor."[21]

For a number of years in the mid-19th century, it even appeared that the water closet might be eclipsed by the earth closet, a device invented in England by the Reverend Henry Moule in 1860. Its major American proponent was George E. Waring, an agricultural engineer who wrote a pamphlet praising the earth closet as cheap, odor free and a superb source of fertilizer for suburban farms. Although Beecher and Stowe — always intrepid reformers of housing design — praised the earth closet in *The American Woman's Home*, the apparent simplicity of water closets won the day. By 1882 Waring had abdicated his advocacy of the earth closet and patented a design for a low water tank with an improved siphonic-jet toilet.[22]

The obvious defects of sheet-metal tubs and water closets — frequent repainting and difficulty in cleaning — led American manufacturers to experiment with cast-iron tubs and hoppers. One of the first was the J. L. Mott Iron Works,

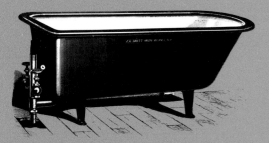

An enameled French bathtub with a wooden rim. From the J. L. Mott Iron Works catalog, 1881.

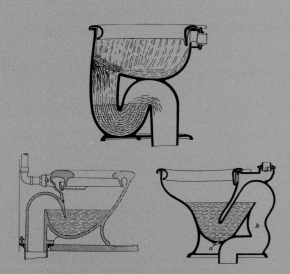

Toilet types developed in the last quarter of the 19th century: the washout, the washdown and the siphonic jet. From Principles and Practice of Plumbing *by J. J. Cosgrove, 1913.*

founded in Mott Haven, N.Y., in 1828. While some of the early cast-iron tubs were encased in wood like their sheet-metal predecessors, a footed, cast-iron bathtub made by the Mott Iron Works appeared in the 1866 catalog of Hayden, Gere and Company of New York. By 1873 the J. L. Mott Iron Works claimed another important first: cast-iron bathtubs with enameled — as opposed to painted — finishes. By 1879 one of its competitors, the Standard Manufacturing Company in Allegheny, Pa., later part of the Standard Sanitary Manufacturing Company, purported to make "one or two" cast-iron tubs a day. Only a few were enameled; most were painted or galvanized.[23] Both companies produced "French pattern" bathtubs that sloped at one end and had piping at the other — a style rapidly adopted in America and one that remains the most common today.

In the meantime, sinks and water closets were improved thanks to advances in the American pottery industry. While English potters were skilled at making sanitary ware such as wash basins and toilet bowls, American potters were not. Ceramic formulas suitable for tableware and bath sets — basins, bowls, slop jars and chamber pots — were not appropriate for heavy sanitary ware. All the sinks and toilet bowls illustrated in the 1881

Mott catalog, for instance, came from Staffordshire.[24] In 1873 Thomas Maddock, who had been trained in china decorating in Staffordshire, became a partner in the Trenton, N.J., pottery firm of Millington and Astbury, and experiments in making basins and toilet bowls began immediately. The earliest attempts yielded less than a 10 percent success rate. For months Maddock walked Lower Manhattan and Brooklyn searching for prospective buyers for the wares that he carried in a bundle weighing nearly 50 pounds. By the end of the year, Maddock had made his first sale, although the customer demanded that he stamp each piece with the words "Best Staffordshire Earthenware made for the American Market."[25] In 1929 Thomas Maddock's Sons Company, successor to the firm Maddock had joined in 1873, became part of the Standard Sanitary Manufacturing Company.[26]

GRADUAL BUT DRAMATIC IMPROVEMENTS

By the 1870s attempts were under way to replace water closets with mechanical parts that controlled the flushing action — such as the pan, valve and plunger types — with new designs in which the action of the water alone flushed the waste and created a seal against sewer

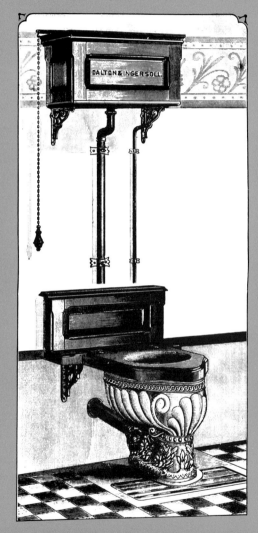

An ornate freestanding, pedestal washout water closet, the Somerset, operated by a pull and chain. The floor flange was brass, and the cistern and seat were available in cherry, ash, walnut, oak or mahogany. From the catalog of Dalton and Ingersoll of Boston, 1889.

gas. "With these," wrote William Paul Gerhard in 1884, "all the machinery is located in the flushing cistern, fixed at a proper height above the water-closet bowl. The water-closet itself is merely a plain bowl — of earthenware in first-class dwellings — with a flushing rim on top of the bowl. . . ."[27] These types of water closets required large amounts of water to rinse both basin and trap thoroughly. Therein lay a problem. All toilet bowls were round, and centrifugal force could thus force the entering water to flow upward, so that a drip tray — ominously called the "save-all tray" — was standard equipment. In 1877 Charles Harrison of New York patented the oval bowl so familiar today. Its shape broke up the centrifugal force and led to the rapid acceptance of the washout, washdown and later the siphonic-jet toilets, the former with high tanks and the latter with a low one.[28] By the late 1880s American potters had perfected the freestanding, pedestal form of water closet, and during the 1890s the wooden tank with a lead or copper liner was replaced by one entirely of vitreous china.

Meanwhile, as the market demand increased, the enamel finishes for cast-iron bathtubs were improved. The first ones had been applied in two stages: a porous base known as a "bone coat" and a sur-face coat mixed with alcohol that was "floated" onto the piece. The process was unsatisfactory because the base coat was often so porous that rust formed and discolored the top glaze.[29] During the early 1880s August Haarlander, the enameling foreman at Standard, and Edward L. Dawes, the manager, began to experiment with enameling by "dredging," a process that resulted in a superior finish and one still used by the industry today. By 1887 Standard was making 10 to 15 bathtubs a day using the improved technique.[30] In that same year, Dawes formed his own company with William A. Myler in New Brighton, Pa. By 1893 business had become so brisk that Dawes and Myler produced only cast-iron enameled bathtubs, and in 1899 the firm became part of the Standard Sanitary Manufacturing Company with Dawes as general manager and Myler as secretary and treasurer. While the interiors of late 19th-century bathtubs received superior enamel finishes, their exteriors continued to be painted.

The J. L. Mott Iron Works took a different approach to the problem by purchasing all-clay, "porcelain" bathtubs from the Trenton Fire Clay and Porcelain Company. The firm, the first in America to produce such tubs, had been formed in 1867 when Oliver Otis Bowman had

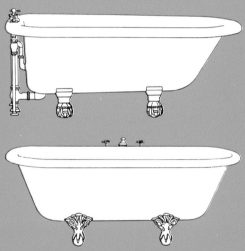

Two porcelain enameled tubs in the French and Roman styles. From Principles and Practice of Plumbing, *1913.*

A common arrangement for bathrooms in city houses toward the end of the 19th century. From Hints on the Drainage and Sewerage of Dwellings, *1884.*

purchased a Trenton company begun in 1845 to make firebricks.[31] Bowman and his sons, Robert and William, first expanded production to include terra-cotta sewer pipe and then experimented with "porcelain" sanitary ware made of fire clay covered with a slip of china followed by a glaze. By 1894 the company manufactured sanitary ware in vitreous china.[32]

Before the Bowmans' success, one-piece ceramic bathtubs had been rare in America because of their cost and difficulty in shipping them from England. Mott, which had begun to import sinks and toilet bowls from England in the

1880s, was certainly aware of these problems and anxious to develop an American manufacture. By 1894 exclusive rights to the Bowmans' production were apparently acquired by the J. L. Mott Iron Works because that was the year the company later claimed to have established its potteries in Trenton. In 1902 the J. L. Mott Iron Works and the Trenton Fire Clay and Porcelain Company merged, with Robert K. Bowman eventually becoming president.[33]

These advances in enamel and porcelain ware dramatically altered the appearance of American bathrooms. While footed bathtubs and three-piece wash-

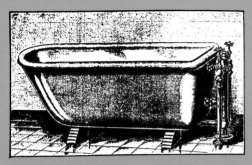

A "crockery" tub of the type made by the Trenton Fire Clay and Porcelain Company. From Lawler's American Sanitary Plumbing, *1896. (Dornsife Collection of The Victorian Society in America)*

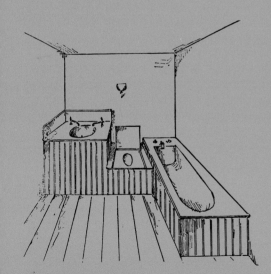

James J. Lawler's idea of a modern bathroom at the turn of the century. From Lawler's American Sanitary Plumbing, *1896. (Dornsife Collection of The Victorian Society in America)*

stands composed of a marble shelf, back splash and porcelain sink continued to be sold well into the 20th century, molded one-piece tubs and sinks were rapidly gaining in popularity. By the last decade of the 19th century, the footed bathtub had come under criticism as posing serious housekeeping problems. The Standard Sanitary Manufacturing Company compared it unfavorably to newer models: "A built-in tub eliminates that accumulation of water and dirt under the back of the tub, which is so difficult to keep clean where the old pattern tub on feet is installed."[34]

THE MODERN BATHROOM

The 1914 catalog of the J. L. Mott Iron Works that is reprinted here illustrated the most fashionable designs in double-shell bathtubs — without feet — and free-standing molded sinks supported by a single pedestal. For $873.05 a home-owner could purchase the "Pan-American" bathroom, whose fixtures consisted of a porcelain, double-shell tub, a shower, a seat bath, a pedestal sink, a bidet and a siphonic-jet toilet. This was the most expensive installation pictured in the catalog; it was equal to a laborer's yearly salary. For $150.25, one could have the "Everett," including a cast-iron tub without feet, enameled on the inside but

painted on the outside, a porcelain sink that attached to the wall and rested on a single leg, and a siphonic-jet toilet. Finally, at $92.75, one could have the "Economic." This, the least stylish of bathrooms, contained an old-fashioned footed bathtub and tubular shower, an enameled sink attached to the wall and a washdown toilet. Clearly, fashion was available — at a price.

Only one footed bathtub appeared in the c. 1935 Standard sales brochure that is reprinted here, and it could be had with a base to give it a look of modernity. The caption described the bathroom containing a footed tub as "Old fashioned — unsightly — an irritation to the family." In comparison, the same room outfitted with a "Neo-Angle bath" was declared "Beautiful — modern — clean — inviting — easy to keep spick and span." The angled bathtub is one surprising feature of this c. 1935 brochure. Its distribution was delayed by the Depression and World War II so that the "Neo-Angle bath" — like most other Art Deco and Moderne furnishings — gained popularity only in the 1950s, 20 years after its debut.

A second surprising feature of the Standard publication — and one with far more lasting impact — was the use of color for bathroom fixtures. Before the

1920s sanitary ware had generally been white with occasional marbleizing or hand-painted decoration. Ceramic tiles, sanitary ("washable") wallpapers and stained-glass windows had given bathrooms their colors. White, however, had remained the dominant part of any color scheme because of its sanitary connotations. By 1935, however, Standard could announce: "The all-white bathroom is no longer favored as the perfect ideal of sanitation."

The Universal Sanitary Manufacturing Company in New Castle, Pa., is credited with pioneering color in sanitary wares in 1926.[35] The Kohler Company of Kohler, Wis., followed in December 1927, announcing a line of six colors: Autumn Brown, Lavender, Spring Green, Old Ivory, West Point Gray and Horizon Blue.[36] These first appeared in Kohler's catalog in 1928, the same year that Crane Plumbing of Chicago, which had earlier experimented with color, introduced a line of 18 colors, six of which were marbleized.[37] By the 1930s Standard fixtures were available in 10 colors that, according to the brochure, had been selected by "an artist of international standing" in order "to compliment the skin" and to provide "a proper basic or key color for correct and livable bathroom color schemes." Correct color schemes could be either analogous or contrasting but "in no case," Standard warned, "should a wall color be chosen that matches the color of the fixtures." No explanation was given for this advice, which is particularly surprising because four of the 10 schemes shown in the 1928 Kohler catalog were monochromatic, with sanitary fixtures and tiles in matching colors.

The J. L. Mott Iron Works did not, apparently, explore color. It had gone into receivership in 1924 and then merged with two other firms in 1927 in a desperate rescue attempt. As the worldwide economic picture darkened and the Depression continued, the company was unable to strengthen its position. Mott went into receivership again in 1931 and closed the following year.[38] When the Standard Sanitary Manufacturing Company encouraged its mid-1930s consumers to "make your bathroom livable" and told them that just "a little extra planning and expenditure [would] develop a room of cheer, of beauty, and extra utility," clearly the modern bathroom had come of age.

RE-CREATING A WELL-APPOINTED BATH

Just as the catalogs reprinted here illustrate that a household's economic standing determined how fully the bathroom might be outfitted, the urban and rural distinctions in plumbing standards also were important. Because buildings usually do not retain their earliest plumbing fixtures, curators of museums seeking to represent the past accurately must take these and other factors into account when planning restorations. Was running water available from a main or an attic cistern? How was waste water disposed of? Where was the bathroom located and how was it illuminated? Was hot water available for bathing and, if so, how was it heated? If old fixtures survive, can they be dated? If the building has been modernized, what might the earliest fixtures have looked like? How were the walls and floors treated? Wood? Tile? Linoleum? Generally speaking, the most up-to-date facilities were available first to prosperous families and urban residents.

Private homeowners, of course, are not subjected to the rigorous authenticity required of museums. For the vast majority of old-house owners, catalogs such as the ones following provide suggestions for an authentic look coupled with modern convenience. As noted earlier, by the early 20th century American manufacturers were able to supply fixtures in styles that included ones still produced today, such as pedestal sinks, porcelain toilets and glazed, cast-iron bathtubs. Furthermore, the J. L. Mott Iron Works catalog shows that by 1914 wooden floors and wainscoting were being supplanted by ceramic tiles in the "best" bathrooms. White fixtures and white tiles — with an occasional colored border — characterized bathroom design until the 1920s. By then, richly colored ceramic tiles had become popular for walls and floors although bathroom fixtures remained white. The first tentative experiments in colored fixtures at the end of the 1920s were all in pastel tones. As illustrated in Standard's sales brochure, these were joined by more intense colors during the 1930s. Like the "Neo-Angle" tub, however, their widespread popularity was delayed until the 1950s.

Contemporary suppliers of fixtures, accessories and tiles that are suitable for late 19th- or early 20th-century bathrooms are listed at the back of this book. When choosing fixtures, it is important to remember that advances in production techniques did not result in wholesale changes in the plumbing industry overnight. Footed bathtubs, for example, were manufactured for at least 80 years. The newest style in the 1860s, they were decidedly old-fashioned by the 1930s, yet one still appeared in the Standard brochure. The Mott and Standard catalogs provide a wealth of information useful in choosing fixtures for period restorations. Together with research and evaluation of current fixtures and accessories, they will help produce a successful re-creation of an early yet well-appointed bath.

1. Melvin M. Rotsch, "The Home Environment," in *Technology in Western Civilization,* ed. by Melvin Kranzberg and Carrol W. Pursell, Jr. (New York: Oxford University Press, 1967), 2:220.

2. Godey's *Lady's Book* 3 (December 1831): 350–51.

3. Harriet Martineau, *Society in America,* 2 vols. (New York: 1837), 2:260.

4. Frances Anne Kemble, *Journal of a Residence on a Georgia Plantation in 1838–1839* (New York: 1863), p. 55.

5. For a study of bathing practices in late 18th- and early 19th-century America, see Richard L. Bushman and Claudia L. Bushman, "The Early History of Cleanliness in America," *Journal of American History* 74 (March 1988): 1213–38.

6. [Eliza Rotch Farrar], *The Young Lady's Friend* (Boston: 1837), pp. 160–61.

7. [Farrar], p. 166.

8. Godey's *Lady's Book* 53 (July 1856): 23.

9. [Farrar], pp. 163–64.

10. Frederick Law Olmsted, *Walks and Talks of an American Farmer in England* (1852), as quoted in *The Horticulturist* 7 (March 1852): 140.

11. Frederick Law Olmsted, *A Journey in the Back Country* (New York: 1860), p. 17.

12. Andrew Jackson Downing, *The Architecture of Country Houses* (1850; reprint ed., New York: Dover Publications, 1969), p. 126.

13. Constance M. Greiff, *John Notman, Architect* (Philadelphia: The Athenaeum of Philadelphia, 1979.), pp. 155–56.

14. Downing, p. 274. For a more detailed description of rams, see Arthur Channing Downs, Jr., "The Introduction of the American Water Ram, ca. 1843–1850," *APT Journal* 7, no. 4 (1975): 56–103, and "The American Water Ram, Part II," *APT Journal* 11, no. 1 (1979): 81–94.

15. Greiff, pp. 156–57.

16. Godey's *Lady's Book* 37 (October 1848): 252.

17. Nicholas B. Wainwright, ed., *A Philadelphia Perspective: The Diary of Sidney George Fisher Covering the Years 1834–1871* (Phildelphia: The Historical Society of Pennsylvania, 1967), pp. 240–41.

18. Godey's *Lady's Book* 92 (April 1876): 386, for the number of bathrooms in Philadelphia in 1876; and Edgar W. Martin, *The Standard of Living in 1860* (Chicago: University of Chicago Press, 1942), p. 112, for the comparison between Philadelphia and New York.

19. Rotsch, 2:217–33. For the development of sewerage systems in the late 19th and early 20th centuries, see Stanley K. Schultz, *Constructing Urban Culture: American Cities and City Planning, 1800–1920* (Philadelphia: Temple University Press, 1989), ch. 7 and 8.

20. Lewis F. Allen, *Rural Architecture* (New York: 1854), pp. 123–24.

21. Catharine Beecher and Harriet Beecher Stowe, *The American Woman's Home* (New York: 1869), p. 38.

22. Beecher and Stowe, pp. 403–18 has a detailed discussion of earth closets complete with illustrations. George E. Waring's patent is cited in Thomas Maddock's Sons Company, *Pottery* (Trenton: 1910), p. 96.

23. E. L. Dawes, "Some Early Experiences in Enameling Cast Iron," in *Bulletin of the American Ceramic Society* (May 1940): 177.

24. According to Thomas Maddock's Sons Company, p. 23, the following four English potteries were responsible for most of the sanitary ware imported into America before 1873: Brown-Westhead-Moore, Twyfords, Brown of Paisley and Dimmock.

25. Thomas Maddock's Sons Company, p. 25.

26. This information furnished courtesy of American Standard, Piscataway, N.J.

27. William Paul Gerhard, *Hints on the Drainage and Sewerage of Dwellings* (New York: 1884), p. 227.

28. Thomas Maddock's Sons Company, pp. 91–96. The first patent issued in America for a jet-action water closet was issued to William Smith of San Francisco in 1876.

29. E. L. Dawes, p. 177.

30. E. L. Dawes, p. 177.

31. Archibald M. Maddock II, *The Polished Earth* (Trenton: 1962), pp. 197–98.

32. "History of the Bowmans," in *Bulletin of the American Ceramic Society* (May 1940): 175.

33. Archibald M. Maddock II, pp. 197–98.

34. Standard Sanitary Manufacturing Company, "Building with Assurance," as quoted in the catalog of Morgan Company, 1921.

35. "Innovation in Plumbing Fixtures Underway," *Domestic Engineering* (October 1981): 157.

36. *Kohler of Kohler News*, December 1927, p. 3.

37. Crane Plumbing Company, *Crane Co. 1855–1975: The First 120 Years* (New York: 1975), p. 23, gives the date of 1928. The company's 1929 catalog, *Homes of Comfort*, illustrates the colors.

38. *New York Times*, 15 December 1927, p. 405, and *Trenton Trentoniana*, 2 June 1932.

J. L. Mott Iron Works

The J. L. Mott Iron Works was organized in 1828 in Mott Haven, N.Y., and remained a family business for five generations. It was an early manufacturer of sanitary equipment, producing soil pipes, brass fittings and enameled ironware. After the Civil War, Mott issued extensive product catalogs that described a wide range of bathroom fixtures, including embossed toilets. Around the turn of the century ceramic and porcelain fixtures were added to the Mott line. These were manufactured by the Trenton Fire Clay and Porcelain Company, a firm begun by Edward Davis in 1845 to produce firebricks. In 1867 this company was acquired by Oliver Otis Bowman who, as O. O. Bowman and Company, also manufactured terra-cotta sewer pipe. Reorganized in 1894 as the Trenton Fire Clay and Porcelain Company, the firm began to manufacture heavy sanitary porcelain ware including the first American all-clay bathtub. In 1902 the J. L. Mott Iron Works merged with the Trenton Fire Clay and Porcelain Company, with all sanitary ware manufactured at Trenton after 1907. Mott began to experience financial difficulties in 1924, went through several receiverships and ceased operation in 1932.

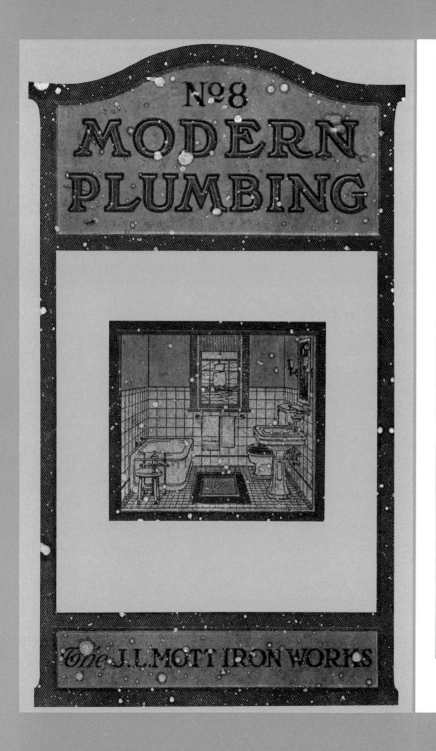

MODERN PLUMBING

NUMBER EIGHT

FIRST EDITION
1914

THE J. L. MOTT IRON WORKS

FIFTH AVE. AND SEVENTEENTH ST.

NEW YORK

PLANT AT TRENTON, N. J.

OUR MANUFACTURING PLANT
ESTABLISHED 1828

OUR manufacturing plant at Trenton, N. J., comprises Potteries, Iron and Brass Foundries, Enameling Works, Cabinet Shops, Ornamental Works, Etc. In 1828 our Works at Mott Haven were established. In 1894 our Potteries were established in Trenton, where, in 1907, our entire manufacturing plant was concentrated.

Not only do we manufacture all the goods we sell, but we manufacture them in

ONE COMPREHENSIVE PLANT

which is undoubtedly one of the most complete and thoroughly equipped of its kind. No expense has been spared to get the very best results in every department, our aim being to produce goods of the highest quality in their various grades, and to do so at a reasonable cost.

The feature of concentration is also of very great importance—manufacturing all our goods in one plant assures the proper assembling and fitting of all component parts, and enables us to make correct and complete shipments.

Main Office and Showroom

FIFTH AVENUE AND SEVENTEENTH STREET
NEW YORK

Showrooms

NEW YORK	BOSTON	CHICAGO	WASHINGTON
DETROIT	ST. LOUIS	DENVER	PHILADELPHIA
SAN FRANCISCO	PITTSBURGH	MONTREAL	PORTLAND, ORE.

Offices

CLEVELAND · MINNEAPOLIS
INDIANAPOLIS · SALT LAKE CITY · ATLANTA
KANSAS CITY · SEATTLE

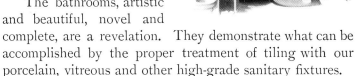

OUR showrooms exemplify the possibilities and perfection of modern plumbing of the highest class, the exhibits being unequaled and eclipsing all our previous efforts.

The bathrooms, artistic and beautiful, novel and complete, are a revelation. They demonstrate what can be accomplished by the proper treatment of tiling with our porcelain, vitreous and other high-grade sanitary fixtures.

It is just as essential for those contemplating building or remodeling their bathrooms to interest themselves in the plumbing fixtures, as it is to select designs of decorations, furnishings, rugs, etc. We therefore strongly urge, that, whenever possible, a visit be paid to our showrooms, where our goods may be examined and their high quality demonstrated.

PREFACE

IN this catalogue we show a large variety of well designed fixtures, thus making it possible for the good taste and individuality of the architect and owner to be reflected in the character of the fixtures chosen. Moreover, the reduced prices of imperial porcelain and vitreous ware make their installation possible, not only in the finest residences, but also in those of moderate cost.

The cost of installation for first-class plumbing fixtures that can be depended upon as giving complete and lasting satisfaction is about the same as for those of the cheaper grade.

Tiling for the bathroom is the most practical as well as the most beautiful material that can be used. Many of our designs are exclusive and cannot be duplicated elsewhere.

The same taste and judgment may be shown in the tiling of a very simple room as for the most elaborate.

It is also essential that the tile shall be set by skilled workmen ; our experience of many years in this particular branch of the tile business has developed a high class of these workers.

THE MODERN BATHROOM

EVOLUTION in the fullest sense of the word is represented by the modern bathrooms as illustrated in this booklet. The utility, the convenience, the sanitary and economic advantages of a well planned, well equipped bathroom are now almost universally acknowledged. Indeed, the house owner and the architect invariably give this the importance and attention which it deserves.

As in the modern hotel each guest is provided with bathroom, so provision is made for guests in the residence. Thus, the modern residence instead of having only one bathroom now usually provides for a bathroom in connection with every sleeping room or suite, and of as large and commodious size as possible. While lavatories and water closets have been improved in many ways, the fixture that has changed the most is the bath. The built-in bath, preferably

of solid porcelain but also of enameled iron, is now almost exclusively used in the private bathroom. Its advantages are many and clearly shown by the varied illustrations in this booklet.

RELATING TO
IMPERIAL PORCELAIN, VITREOUS PORCELAIN AND
ENAMELED IRON PLUMBING FIXTURES

FOR the best plumbing work, imperial and vitreous solid porcelain fixtures are in a class by themselves, nothing else being at all comparable either for beauty, cleanliness or durability.

Clay products after going through a drying process covering four or five weeks, are placed in the kiln where they remain for about ten days subjected to a heat running up to 2500 degrees.

2500 **DEGREES OF HEAT** fuse the vitreous glaze integral with the clay body of the bath, thereby insuring a glaze and a hardness of surface unattainable in the

enamel on cast iron for the obvious reason that the latter can only be fired at a very much lower heat, consequently the softer surface of the enamel cannot be so easily kept clean or free from stains as the porcelain, *i. e.*, by simply wiping with a cloth or sponge.

PROCESS OF ENAMELING THE CAST-IRON BATH

After the bath is cast, the enamel is applied. The bath is then placed in enameling oven where it is subjected to about 1800 degrees of heat

WE fully recognize that enameled ironware, or porcelain-enameled ware as it is usually catalogued, of which we are the oldest makers, will continue to be a considerable factor in plumbing fixtures, especially the enameled iron bath tub, which, until the advent of the solid porcelain tub, was the bath *par excellence*, and doubtless will continue to be largely used in medium and cheaper class of work; only, we desire it to be well understood just what *porcelain ware* is and what *enameled ironware is*, so that the purchaser may not make a mistake or be misled by a similarity of terms. The bath tub has always been the most successful enameled iron fixture, *i. e.*, when compared with lavatories and sinks, for the simple reason that it is not subjected to the same usage; used only for bathing purposes, it is less likely to be stained or chipped and should, with ordinary care, be very satisfactory.

Plate 1101-A, Bathroom "Valcour"

THIS interior shows a group of recent designs, with harmonious setting of tiled floor and walls. Left of the doorway is a needle and shower bath with water-tight plate-glass door. On the right, a linen closet serves also for the concealed bath fittings.

This combination of porcelain, tile and glass may easily be kept in spotless condition.

In design and treatment the tile is modern English.

Price of fixtures in this bathroom ranges from $724.75 to $826.75; for details, see next page.

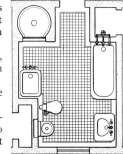

MINIMUM SIZE, 13' X 9' 6"

Plate 1101-A, Bathroom "Valcour"

	Imp. Porc.	
	Class A	Class B

Bath—The "Plaza" imperial porcelain, glazed outside white, with "Pembroke" supply and waste fittings (concealed waste and bell supply, ¾" compression valves with 4-arm china handles and china escutcheons),

5' x 2' 8" x 17" deep	$154 75	$133 75
Same, 5' 6" x 2' 8" x 17" deep . . .	175 75	144 25
Same, 6' x 2' 8" x 17" deep	241 00	193 75

For details of "Pembroke" bath fittings, see page 29.

Note—When ordering, state if fittings are to be at right or left end as you face the bath.

Seat Bath—The "Latona" imperial porcelain, glazed outside white, with n. p. "Unique" supply and waste fittings with 4-arm china handles 104 00   75 50

Note—When ordering, state if fittings are to be at right or left end as you face the bath.

Shower—The "Regent" n. p. combination needle and shower bath, with 10½" tubular shower head, n. p. compression valves, check valves, testing valve, lock shield graduated control valves to wall (one n. p. key included in price of combination), imperial porcelain receptor (39" x 40"), plate-glass door with n. p. frame and handle, and n. p. 5" waste strainer with 3" coupling . . 415 75   381 75

Lavatory—The "Valcour" with pedestal, n. p. compression "Primus" combination supply and waste (4-arm china handles with china name-plates) and 1½"

			Vit. Porc.
n. p. half S trap with i. p. size waste to wall, 30" x 24".	76 50	58 00	$76 50
Same, 33" x 24"	81 75	62 00	81 75
Same, 36" x 24"	89 50	68 50	89 50

Note—China escutcheons for "Primus" combination same price as n. p.

Dental—Vitreous porcelain lavatory; for description and price, see subsequent pages.

Water Closet—The "Langham" syphon-jet with n. p. "Presto" valve, adjustable shut-off valve, seat and cover with No. 1 cellu-enamel white finish, and the sanitary-perfect screw connection . . . 75 75

Same, with cabinet finish quartered oak seat and cover 66 25

Imperial porcelain floor slab, extra . . . 3 50

Furnishings—See subsequent pages.

Tiling—Prices of tiling, set and unset, on application. Diagram of room should accompany inquiry.

For separate illustrations of baths, lavatories, closets and bidets, see subsequent pages.

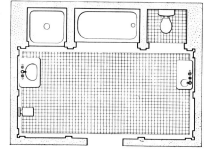

Plate 1103-A, Bathroom "Prescott"

THIS interior gives an idea of what can be accomplished by treating the bathrooms as an architectural problem—*building* appropriate fixtures into the room with appropriate tiling, instead of merely *arranging* them on the floor.

Such a room would be a distinguishing feature in the finest home.

Tiling—The tiling is exclusively our own design, the tint being a delicate ivory white finish.

Price of fixtures in this bathroom ranges from $688.50 to $821.25; for details, see next page.

MINIMUM SIZE, 15' X 9'

Plate 1103-A, Bathroom "Prescott"

	Imp. Porc.	
	Class A	Class B

Bath—The "**Prescott**" imperial porcelain, glazed outside white, with "**Pembroke**" supply and waste fittings (concealed waste and bell supply, ¾" compression valves with 4-arm china handles and china escutcheons), n. p. combination shower valves (for ½" i. p.), shower, offset curtain rod with white duck curtain, chain and hook, 5' x 2' 8" x 19" deep . . $276 00 $221 75

Same, 5' 6" x 2' 8" x 19" deep 302 25 233 50

Same, 6' x 2' 8" x 19" deep 354 75 280 75

For details of "**Pembroke**" bath fittings, see page 29.

Note — When ordering, state if fittings are to be at right or left end as you face the bath.

Shower—The "**Regent**" n. p. combination needle and shower bath, with 10½" tubular shower head, n. p. compression valves, check valves, testing valve, lock shield graduated control valves to wall (one n. p. key included in price), with white duck curtain, offset curtain rod and snaps, soap dish, imperial porcelain receptor (39" x 40"), and n. p. 5" waste strainer with 3" coupling 286 25 252 25

| | | | Vit. Porc. |

Lavatory—The "**Valcour**" with pedestal, n. p. No. 2 "**Primus**" combination supply and waste with china handles, and 1½" n. p. half S trap with i. p. size waste to wall, 30" x 24" 73 25 54 75 $73 25

Same, 33" x 24" 78 50 58 75 78 50

Same, 36" x 24" 86 25 65 25 86 25

Water Closet—The "**Silentis**" syphon-jet, seat and cover with No. 1 cellu-enamel white finish, n. p. bar hinge, No. 72 vitreous porcelain cistern with china push-button and the sanitary-perfect screw connection . 79 25

Same, with cabinet finish quartered oak seat and cover with n. p. bar hinge 70 75

Imperial porcelain floor slab, extra . . . 3 50

Supply pipe, n. p. (i. p. size) to floor with stop valve, less union, extra, $2.00. Same, less stop valve, $1.00.

Toilet Table—The "**Newport**" imperial porcelain with manicure bowl, painted iron frame, wall supports with china escutcheons and imperial porcelain pedestals, n. p. No. 2 "**Primus**" combination supply and waste with china handles and 1½" n. p. half S trap with i. p. size waste to wall 106 50 80 50

Prices of mirrors with tile frames furnished on application.

Furnishings—See subsequent pages.

Brass Work—n. p. indicates nickel-plated brass work.

Tiling—Prices of tiling, set and unset, on application. Diagram of room should accompany inquiry.

For separate illustrations of baths, lavatories and closets, see subsequent pages.

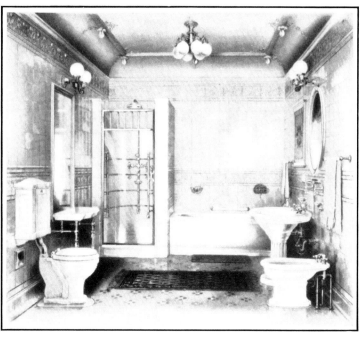

Plate 1105-A, Bathroom "Duval"

BY introducing a tile partition, as above, a built-in porcelain bath can be installed in connection with a needle and shower bath, the partition forming one side of the bath recess. The needle and shower bath has a plate-glass door, making the shower recess practically water-tight. Real bathing luxury, with unusual economy of space.

Tiling—The design is pure Italian renaissance, delicately tinted in four colors, with ¼″ border lines in gold; or, if preferred, it may be white and gold, or plain white throughout. The medicine cabinet is set in the tile.

Price of fixtures in this bathroom ranges from $781.80 to $851.55; for details, see next page.

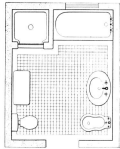

MINIMUM SIZE, 11′ 6″ x 9′

Plate 1105-A, Bathroom "Duval"

	Imp. Porc.	
	Class A	Class B
Bath—The "**Empress**" imperial porcelain, glazed outside white, with "**Pallas**" supply and waste fittings (concealed waste and bell supply, n. p. ⅝″ compression valves with n. p. escutcheons), 5′ x 2′ 8″ x 17″ deep .	$144 00	$123 00
Same, 5′ 6″ x 2′ 8″ x 17″ deep . . .	165 00	133 50
Same, 6′ x 2′ 8″ x 17″ deep	230 25	183 00
If with 4-arm china handles on supply valves, add .	2 50	

Note—China escutcheons for "Pallas" bath fittings, extra, $0.75.

The "Pallas" supply valves measure 3″ from face of wall to center of valves and are tapped for ¾″ iron pipe. In a thicker wall the valves can be partially or entirely buried. The valves, however, cannot be lengthened.

Note—When ordering, state if fittings are to be at right or left end as you face the bath.

	Class A	Class B	
Shower—The "**Regent**" n. p. combination needle and shower bath with 10½″ tubular shower head, n. p. compression valves, check valves, testing valve, lock shield graduated control valves to wall (one n. p. key included in price of combination), soap dish, imperial porcelain receptor (39″ x 40″), plate-glass door with n. p. frame and handle, and n. p. 5″ waste strainer with 3″ coupling	418 75	384 75	

			Vit. Porc.
Lavatory—The "**Victorian**" with pedestal, n. p. compression "**Primus**" combination supply and waste (n. p. 5-ball handles with china name-plates) and 1½″ n. p. half S trap with i. p. size waste to wall, 27″ x 22″	64 75	55 50	$64 75
Same, 32″ x 24″	76 25	59 25	76 25
Same, 37″ x 27″	86 75	67 25	
Mirror—Beveled plate glass with 2⅜″ polished wood frame, finished in white enamel, 33″ x 24″ . .	25 25		
Same, 36″ x 27″	29 50		
Water Closet—The "**Silentis**" syphon-jet, seat and cover with No. 1 cellu-enamel white finish, n. p. bar hinge, No. 72 vitreous porcelain cistern with china push-button and the sanitary-perfect screw connection .	79 25		
Same, with cabinet finish quartered oak seat and cover with n. p. bar hinge	70 75		
Imperial porcelain floor slab, extra . . .	3 50		

Supply pipe, n. p. (i. p. size) to floor with stop valve, less union, extra, $2.00. Same, less stop valve, $1.00.

Bidet—The "**Duval**" all porcelain flushing-rim with n. p. combination hot and cold supply to jet and flushing-rim with n. p. rose spray and jet, n. p. "**Unique**" waste and supply pipes to floor	59 80		
Imperial porcelain floor slab, extra . . .	3 50		
Toilet Table—Imperial porcelain, with brass frame .	45 00	39 50	
Mirror—Beveled plate glass, with 1⅝″ white enameled wood frame, 54″ x 30″	40 00		

Plate 1107-A, Bathroom "Pan-American"

A VERY completely equipped bathroom which is practically a reproduction of our exhibit which received the highest award at the Paris and Pan-American Expositions. A special feature is the corner needle and shower with tiled walls and plate-glass door. In use, the water is kept within bounds while the temperature is indicated and controlled by a new device.

Tiling—The design is "Renaissance" delicately tinted; or if preferred, it may be white and gold.

Price of fixtures in this bathroom ranges from $769.80 to $873.05; for details, see next page.

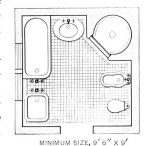

MINIMUM SIZE, 9' 6" X 9'

Plate 1107-A, Bathroom "Pan-American"

	Imp. Porc. Class A	Class B	Vit. Porc.
Bath—The "**La Salle**" imperial porcelain, glazed outside white, with n. p. "**Unique**" supply and waste fittings, 5' x 2' 8" x 17" deep	$150 00	$118 50	
Same, 5' 6" x 2' 8" x 17" deep	160 50	129 00	
Same, 6' x 2' 8" x 17" deep	212 50	165 25	
If with 4-arm china handles on supply valves, add	2 50		

Note—When ordering, state if fittings are to be at right or left end as you face the bath.

The "**Unique**" bath fittings are extra heavy and have ¾" valves and supplies.

Shower—The "**Perry**" n. p. combination needle and shower bath with 10½" tubular shower head, n. p. compression valves, check valves, testing valve, lock shield graduated control valves to wall (one n. p. key included in price of combination), imperial porcelain receptor (42"), plate-glass door with n. p. frame and handle, and n. p. 5" waste strainer with 3" coupling	407 25	373 25	
Seat Bath—The "**Latona**" imperial porcelain, glazed outside white, with n. p. "**Unique**" supply and waste fittings, 2' 5" x 2' 1"	101 50	73 00	

Note—When ordering, state if fittings are to be at right or left end as you face the bath.

Lavatory—The "**Victorian**" with pedestal, n. p. compression "**Primus**" combination supply and waste (n. p. 5-ball handles with china name-plates) and 1½" n. p. half S trap with i. p. size waste to wall, 27" x 22"	64 75	55 50	$64 75
Same, 32" x 24"	76 25	59 25	76 25
Same, 37" x 27"	86 75	67 25	
If with 4-arm china handles instead of n. p. 5-ball handles, add	2 50		
Mirror—Beveled plate glass (colonial design) with white enameled 3¼" wood frame, 33" x 24"	31 00		
Same, 36" x 27"	36 00		
Medicine Cabinet—Recessed, with white enameled wood frame touched with gold, beveled mirror and two adjustable plate-glass shelves	80 00		
Water Closet—The "**Silentis**" syphon-jet, seat and cover with No. 1 cellu-enamel white finish, n. p. bar hinge, No. 33 design L cellu-enamel (white) cistern with No. 1 n. p. brass brackets, flush pipe, No. 2 guide, rod, links and china pull, and the sanitary-perfect screw connection	89 75		
Same, with cabinet finish quartered oak seat, cover and cistern	66 75		
Bidet—The "**Duval**" all porcelain flushing-rim with n. p. combination hot and cold supply to jet and flushing-rim with n. p. rose spray and jet, n. p. "**Unique**" waste and supply pipes to floor	59 80		
If bidet is furnished with fittings for cold water only, deduct	3 95		

Plate 1109-A, Bathroom " Renaissance "

IN the handling of a bathroom interior, the tiling may be designed to conform with any style of decoration. Above is shown a classical treatment of panels divided by pilasters so arranged as to frame in the mirrors and windows. We are equipped not only to design such interiors but to produce the tile and to attend to every detail of its setting.

Tiling—The tile used in this interior is special and of our own design.

Price of fixtures in this bathroom ranges from $316.25 to $363.50; for details, see next page.

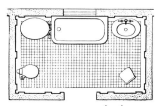

MINIMUM SIZE, 12′ X 7′

Plate 1109-A, Bathroom " Renaissance "

	Imp. Porc.		
	Class A	Class B	
Bath—The "Vernon" imperial porcelain, glazed outside white, with n. p. "Eton" supply and waste fittings, with china handles, 5′ x 2′ 8″ x 17″ deep	$173 75	$150 75	
Same, 5′ 6″ x 2′ 8″ x 17″ deep	197 00	162 25	
Same, 6′ x 2′ 8″ x 17″ deep	269 50	217 75	

For details of "Eton" bath fittings, see page 23.

Note—When ordering, state if fittings are to be at right or left end as you face the bath.

			Vit. Porc.
Lavatory—The "Victorian" with pedestal, n. p. No. 2 "Primus" combination supply and waste with china handles, and 1½″ n. p. half S trap with i. p. size waste to wall, 27″ x 22″	64 00	54 75	$64 00
Same, 32″ x 24″	75 50	58 50	75 50
Same, 37″ x 27″	86 00	66 50	

Water Closet—The "Langham" syphon-jet with n. p. "Presto" flush valve, adjustable shut-off valve, seat and cover with No. 1 cellu-enamel white finish and the sanitary-perfect screw connection	75 75	
Same, with cabinet finish quartered oak seat and cover	66 25	

The sanitary-perfect screw connection effects a permanently tight joint between the closet and soil pipe, thus preventing the possibility of sewer gas escaping at this point.

Toilet Table—Imperial porcelain, oval, with imperial porcelain fluted pedestal	50 00	35 00
Same, with plain pedestal	39 00	26 00

Medicine Cabinets—Two, colonial, with white enameled wood frame and leaded glass doors and eight adjustable plate-glass shelves	160 00
Paper Holder—Cellu-enamel with drawer and cabinet	20 00

Prices of mirrors with tile frames furnished on application.

Furnishings—See subsequent pages.

Brass Work—n. p. indicates nickel-plated brass work.

Tiling—Prices of tiling, set and unset, on application. Diagram of room should accompany inquiry.

For separate illustrations of baths, lavatories and closets, see subsequent pages.

Plate IIII-A, Bathroom "Art Nouveau"

ANOTHER interior from our Fifth Avenue showrooms, illustrating the possibilities of specially designed tiling to secure unusual effects in bathroom treatment. The tile design on walls is executed in a delicate gray with floor of stone mosaic in corresponding pattern. All fixtures are of solid porcelain.

Price of fixtures in this bathroom ranges from $492.50 to $617.75; for details, see next page.

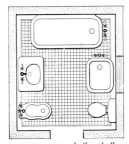

MINIMUM SIZE, 8' 6" X 7' 6"

Plate IIII-A, Bathroom "Art Nouveau"

	Imp. Porc.	
	Class A	Class B

Bath—The "**Grantham**" imperial porcelain, glazed outside white, with n. p. "**Eton**" supply and waste fittings with china handles, 5' 7" x 2' 8" x 19" deep . . $277 00 $198 75

The "**Eton**" fittings are regularly furnished with ¾" valves and supplies.

If with 1" valves and supplies and extra large waste, add . . 21 00

The "**Eton**" bath fittings with the china handles on valves and waste are very handsome. A quarter turn of the handle opens the valves and likewise closes them. For ordinary pressure the Fuller valves are most satisfactory, but for high pressure we advise using the compression, see page 18.

Note—When ordering, state if fittings are to be at right or left end as you face the bath.

Shower—n. p. tubular shower with 8½" tubular shower head n. p. combination shower valves, curved curtain rod, white duck curtain, chain and hook . . 45 75

Seat Bath—The "**Latona**" imperial porcelain, glazed outside white, with n. p. "**Eton**" supply and waste fittings with china handles 103 75 75 25

Note—When ordering, state if fittings are to be at right or left end as you face the bath.

Lavatory—The "**Valcour**" with pedestal, n. p. No. 3 "**Primus**" combination supply and waste with china handles, and 1½" n. p. half S trap with i. p. size waste to wall, 30" x 24" . . . . . . [Vit. Porc.]

			Vit. Porc.
to wall, 30" x 24"	74 00	55 50	$74 00
Same, 33" x 24"	79 00	59 50	79 00
Same, 36" x 24"	87 00	66 00	87 00

Mirrors—Two beveled plate glass, with 1⅝" polished wood frames, finished in white enamel, 54" x 30" . . . 80 00

Water Closet—The "**Silentis**" syphon-jet, seat and cover with No. 1 cellu-enamel white finish, n. p. bar hinge, No. 77 vitreous porcelain cistern with china lever handle and the sanitary-perfect screw connection . 68 75

Same, with cabinet finish quartered oak seat and cover and n. p. bar hinge 60 25

Imperial porcelain floor slab, extra . . . 3 50

Supply pipe, n. p. (i. p. size) to floor with stop valve, less union, extra, $2.00. Same, less stop valve, $1.00.

Bidet—The "**Durward**" all-porcelain flushing-rim, with n. p. combination hot and cold mixing valves to bidet and flushing-rim, and n. p. "**Nassau**" waste . . 48 50

Imperial porcelain floor slab, extra . . . 3 50

Furnishings—See subsequent pages.

Brass Work—n. p. indicates nickel-plated brass work.

Tiling—Prices of tiling, set and unset, on application. Diagram of room should accompany inquiry.

For separate illustrations of baths, lavatories, closets and bidets, see subsequent pages.

Plate 1114-A, Bathroom "Baronial"

GOOD housekeepers appreciate the advantages of a built-in bath, such as is shown above. Installed with the utmost economy of space, there are no awkward places beneath or behind it to keep clean. The bath is glazed inside and out giving it a beautiful china white surface which can be kept spotless by wiping with a cloth or sponge. The combination in this interior of the oval lavatory mirror and fittings is extremely appropriate.

Tiling—The frieze is an elongated leaf pattern in high relief. It is usually preferred in plain white or white touched with green.

Price of fixtures in this bathroom ranges from $603.75 to $709.50; for details, see next page.

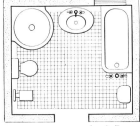

MINIMUM SIZE, 9' X 7' 6"

Plate 1114-A, Bathroom "Baronial"

	Imp. Porc. Class A	Class B
Bath—The "Baronial" imperial porcelain, glazed outside white, with n. p. "Eton" supply and waste fittings with china handles, 5' x 2' 8" x 19" deep .	$219 50	$165 25
Same, 5' 6" x 2' 8" x 19" deep . . .	245 75	177 00
Same, 6' x 2' 8" x 19" deep	298 25	224 25

For details of "Eton" bath fittings, see page 23.

Note—When ordering, state if fittings are to be at right or left end as you face the bath.

Shower—n. p. needle and shower bath with white duck curtain, soap dish, imperial porcelain corner receptor set into wall with n. p. 5" waste strainer with 3" coupling	293 00	255 00
If with n. p. "Thermo" mixing valve, add . .	22 75	

Diameter of receptor outside, 45"; inside, 39"; projection from corner, 53"; depth inside, 5½"; height, 7¾"; width of roll rim, 3"

	Imp. Porc. Class A	Class B	Vit. Porc.
Lavatory—The "Nouveau" with pedestal, n. p. No. 2 "Primus" combination supply and waste with china handles and 1½" n. p. half S trap with i. p. size waste to wall, 27" x 22"	64 00	54 75	$64 00
Same, 32" x 24"	75 50	58 50	75 50
Same, 37" x 27"	86 00	66 50	

Mirror—Beveled plate glass (oval colonial design) with polished wood frame finished in white enamel, 33" x 24"	31 00	
Same, 36" x 27"	36 00	

Water Closet—The "Silentis" syphon-jet, seat and cover with No. 1 cellu-enamel white finish, n. p. bar hinge, No. 74 vitreous porcelain cistern with china lever handle and the sanitary-perfect screw connection .	68 75	
Same, with cabinet finish quartered oak seat and cover with n. p. bar hinge	60 25	
Imperial porcelain floor slab, extra	3 50	

Supply pipe, n. p. (i. p. size) to floor with stop valve, less union, extra, $2.00. Same, less stop valve, $1.00.

Bathroom Seat—Imperial porcelain, with imperial porcelain standard and wall supports	24 25	20 00

Mirror—Beveled plate glass with polished wood frame, finished in white enamel, 54" x 30"	40 00	

Tiling—Prices of tiling, set and unset, on application. Diagram of room should accompany inquiry.

For separate illustrations of baths, lavatories and closets, see subsequent pages.

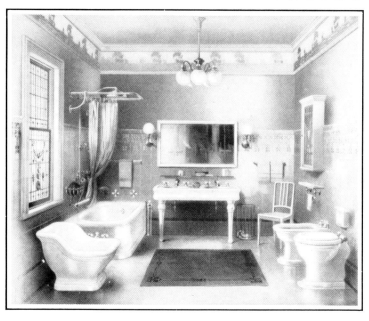

Plate 1116-A, Bathroom "Pierpont"

WHEN choosing bathroom equipment, material as well as design should be considered. Here is a very complete group of solid porcelain fixtures — the finest material known to sanitary science. They are beautiful in design and can be kept spotless by wiping with a cloth or sponge. Of special interest is the extra long lavatory with two basins. The seat bath and bidet are modern conveniences too little considered in planning bathrooms.

Price of fixtures in this bathroom ranges from $550.25 to $662.00; for details, see next page.

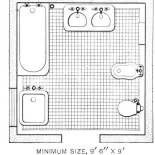

MINIMUM SIZE, 9' 6" X 9'

Plate 1116-A, Bathroom "Pierpont"

	Imp. Porc. Class A	Imp. Porc. Class B
Bath—The "**Pierpont**" imperial porcelain, glazed outside white, with n. p. "**Penroy**" fittings (standing waste through floor with brace to wall, n. p. bell supply and n. p. ¾" compression valves in wall with 4-arm china handles and n. p. escutcheons), 5' x 2' 8" x 19" deep.	$218 25	$164 00
Same, 5' 6" x 2' 8" x 19" deep	244 50	175 75
Same, 6' x 2' 8" x 19" deep	297 00	223 00

For details of "**Penroy**" supply valves, see page 29.

Note—When ordering, state if fittings are to be at right or left end as you face the bath.

Shower—n. p. shower and shampoo, with 8½" tubular shower head, curtain ring, white duck curtain, chain and hook and n. p. supply pipes to wall with check valves .	56 00	
If with n. p. "**Thermo**" mixing valve, add . . .	13 75	
Seat Bath—The "**Latona**" imperial porcelain with n. p. "**Unique**" supply and waste fittings with 4-arm china handles	104 00	75 50

Note—When ordering, state if fittings are to be at right or left end as you face the bath.

Lavatory—The "**Clinton**" imperial porcelain with imperial porcelain legs, wall supports, n. p. compression "**Primus**" supplies and wastes (4-arm china handles with china name-plates) and 1½" n. p. half S traps with i. p. size nipples to wall, 4' 2" x 2' 1"	159 50	130 50
Mirror—Beveled plate glass with 3¼" white enameled wood frame, 48" x 30"	44 00	
Medicine Cabinet—Colonial, with white enameled wood frame and leaded glass door and two adjustable plate-glass shelves	80 00	
Water Closet—The "**Langham**" syphon-jet with n. p. "**Presto**" flush valve, adjustable shut-off valve, seat and cover with No. 1 cellu-enamel white finish and the sanitary-perfect screw connection . . .	75 75	
Same, with cabinet finish quartered oak seat and cover	66 25	
Imperial porcelain floor slab, extra	3 50	
Bidet—The "**Durward**" all porcelain flushing-rim with n. p. combination hot and cold mixing valves to bidet and flushing-rim, and n. p. "**Nassau**" waste . .	48 50	
Imperial porcelain floor slab, extra	3 50	

Furnishings—See subsequent pages.

Brass Work—n. p. indicates nickel-plated brass work.

Tiling—Prices of tiling, set and unset, on application. Diagram of room should accompany inquiry.

The tiling in this interior is modern English in character, and of our own design, in two soft contrasting tints.

For separate illustrations of baths, lavatories and closets, see subsequent pages.

Plate 1118-A, Bathroom "Plaza"

THIS is one of the 600 bathrooms furnished for the "Plaza", one of the finest of New York's magnificent hotels. Experienced hotel men have learned that solid porcelain fixtures are more economical than any other kind when compared on the basis of initial cost, plus servant's time, plus the cost of upkeep. On this strictly business basis, the leading modern hotels have been equipped with Mott's fixtures.

Tiling—The bathrooms in the Plaza Hotel are tiled as shown above, the panel tile being either green, drab or brown.

Price of fixtures in this bathroom ranges from $267.00 to $306.25; for details, see next page.

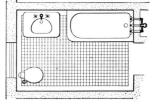

MINIMUM SIZE, 8' 6" X 6'

Plate 1118-A, Bathroom "Plaza"

	Imp. Porc. Class A	Class B	
Bath—The "Plaza" imperial porcelain, glazed outside white, with "Pembroke" supply and waste fittings (concealed waste and bell supply, ¾" compression valves with 4-arm china handles and china escutcheons), 5' x 2' 8" x 17" deep	$154 75	$133 75	
Same, 5' 6" x 2' 8" x 17" deep	175 75	144 25	
Same, 6' x 2' 8" x 17" deep	241 00	193 75	

The "Pembroke" and "Penroy" supply valves are regularly furnished measuring 3" from face of wall to center of valves and are tapped for ¾" iron pipe. This distance of 3" can be increased at an additional cost.

Note—China escutcheons for "Pembroke" and "Penroy" bath fittings same price as n. p.

The "Pembroke" bath fittings are concealed in pipe shaft or adjoining closet where they are accessible for repairs. Where either of the above plans is not feasible, the "Penroy" fittings, as shown in Plate 1116-A, page 26, may be substituted.

Note—When ordering, state if fittings are to be at right or left end as you face the bath.

			Vit. Porc.
Lavatory—The "Valando" with legs, china wall supports, n. p. compression "Primus" combination supply and waste (4-arm china handles with china name-plates) and 1½" n. p. half S trap with i. p. size waste to wall, 30" x 24"	75 75	57 50	$75 75
Same, 33" x 24"	81 00	61 25	81 00
Same, 36" x 24"	88 75	67 75	88 75
Same, 42" x 24"	99 75	80 75	99 75
Water Closet—The "Langham" syphon-jet with n. p. "Presto" flush valve, adjustable shut-off valve, seat and cover with No. 1 cellu-enamel white finish and the sanitary-perfect screw connection . . .	75 75		
Same, with cabinet finish quartered oak seat and cover	66 25		
Imperial porcelain floor slab, extra . . .	3 50		

Prices of mirrors with tile frames furnished on application.

Furnishings—See subsequent pages.

Brass Work—n. p. indicates nickel-plated brass work.

Tiling—Prices of tiling, set and unset, on application. Diagram of room should accompany inquiry.

Plate 1120-A, Bathroom "Empress"

THIS is a reproduction of one of 11 bathrooms, which may be seen at our Fifth Avenue showrooms in New York. These model rooms give an idea of the range and possibilities of modern bathroom equipment that can be gained in no other way. This interior is a fine example of what can be accomplished in a comparatively restricted space.

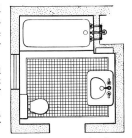

MINIMUM SIZE, 7' X 6'

Tiling—The walls are of white glazed tile with two tinted ½" ribbon tiles set near top and 1" near bottom. The floor is 1" glazed or unglazed vitreous tile.

Price of fixtures in this bathroom ranges from $308.50 to $348.00; for details, see next page.

Plate 1120-A, Bathroom "Empress"

	Imp. Porc.	
	Class A	Class B

Bath—The "**Empress**" imperial porcelain, glazed outside white, with n. p. "**Pallas**" supply and waste fittings, (concealed waste and bell supply, n. p. ⅝" compression valves with 4-arm china handles and n. p. escutcheons),

	Class A	Class B
5' x 2' 8" x 17" deep	$146 50	$125 50
Same, 5' 6" x 2' 8" x 17" deep	167 50	136 00
Same, 6' x 2' 8" x 17" deep	232 75	185 50

Note—China escutcheons for "**Pallas**" bath fittings, extra, $0.75.

For details of "**Pallas**" bath fittings, see page 17.

Note—When ordering, state if fittings are to be at right or left end as you face the bath.

Shower—n. p. tubular shower with 8½" tubular shower head, n. p. combination shower valves, curved curtain rod, white duck curtain, chain and hook . . . 45 75

Lavatory—The "**Valcour**" with pedestal, n. p. compression "**Primus**" combination supply and waste (4-arm china handles with china name-plates) and 1½" n. p. half S trap with i. p. size waste to wall,

			Vit. Porc.
30" x 24"	76 50	58 00	$76 50
Same, 33" x 24"	81 75	62 00	81 75
Same, 36" x 24"	89 50	68 50	89 50

Mirror—Beveled plate glass with 2⅜" polished wood frame, finished in white enamel, 33" x 24" . . . 17 25

Water Closet—The "**Silentis**" syphon-jet, seat and cover with No. 1 cellu-enamel white finish, n. p. bar hinge, No. 72 vitreous porcelain cistern with china push-button and the sanitary-perfect screw connection . . 79 25

Same with cabinet finish quartered oak seat and cover with n. p. bar hinge . . . 70 75

Imperial porcelain floor slab, extra . . . 3 50

Supply pipe, n. p. (i. p. size) to floor with stop valve, less union, extra, $2.00. Same, less stop valve, $1.00.

The "**Silentis**" is the ideal water closet for the modern residence. By an ingenious arrangement of the supply to the bowl and syphon-jet, the noise of flushing is reduced to a minimum. Running water cannot further be silenced and still produce a sanitary flush.

Other salient features of the "**Silentis**" are the extra large bowl and seat; concealed jet holes; drain plug which allows removing of water from the bowl without disturbing the soil connection, and the sanitary-perfect screw connection (patented), insuring a permanently tight joint between the closet and soil pipe.

Tiling—Prices of tiling, set and unset, on application. Diagram of room should accompany inquiry.

For separate illustrations of baths, lavatories and closets, see subsequent pages.

Plate 1122-A, Bathroom "Granada"

A SUGGESTION for convenient isolation of the closet from the main bathroom with access from hall and bathroom.   The bath shown above is of extra length—a genuine luxury where space need not be considered.   The seat bath is a valuable fixture where space permits—at once a special comfort and a saving of time and of water.

Tiling—The frieze is of a delicate empire-colonial design in white and gold or tinted. The window casing and frame of the door to toilet room are of molded tile.

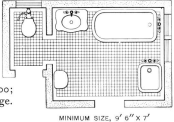

MINIMUM SIZE, 9′ 6″ x 7′

Price of fixtures in this bathroom ranges from $479.00 to $584.00; for details, see next page.

Plate 1122-A, Bathroom "Granada"

	Imp. Porc.	
	Class A	Class B
Bath—The "Granada" imperial porcelain, glazed outside white, with n. p. "Eton" supply and waste fittings with china handles, 5′ 6″ x 2′ 8″ x 19″ deep	$224 75	$167 00
Same, 6′ x 3′ 4″ x 19″ deep	471 50	332 00

For details of "Eton" bath fittings, see page 39.

Note—When ordering, state if fittings are to be at right or left end as you face the bath.

Shower—n. p. tubular shower with 8½″ tubular shower head, with rubber-bound shampoo, 25″ curtain ring, white duck curtain, chain and hook, and n. p. supply pipes to wall with check valves 45 25

Seat Bath—The "Latona" imperial porcelain, glazed outside white, with n. p. "Eton" supply and waste fittings with china handles . . . . 103 75 . 75 25

Note—When ordering, state if fittings are to be at right or left end as you face the bath.

Lavatory—The "Norwood" with pedestal, n. p. No. 2 "Primus" combination supply and waste with china handles, and 1½″ n. p. half S trap with i. p. size waste to wall, 27″ x 23″			Vit. Porc.
	72 25	57 75	$72 25
Same, 30″ x 23″	77 25	59 00	77 25
Same, 34″ x 25″	89 00	65 50	89 00

If with n. p. compression "Primus" combination (as Plate 4024-A, page 76), add 0 75

Mirror—Beveled plate glass with 2⅜″ wood frame, finished in white enamel, 30″ x 24″ . . . 23 50
Same, 36″ x 27″ 32 25

Water Closet—The "Prompto" syphon-jet with n. p. No. 2 "Simplex" flush and stop valve, No. 6 seat and cover with No. 2 cellu-enamel white finish, n. p. bar hinge and the sanitary-perfect screw connection . 51 75
Same, with No. 6 cabinet finish quartered oak seat and cover with n. p. bar hinge 46 00
Imperial porcelain floor slab, extra . . . 3 50

Bathroom Seat—Imperial porcelain with imperial porcelain standard and wall supports . . . . 24 25 . 20 00

Mirror—Beveled plate glass (over seat), with 2⅜″ wood frame, finished in white enamel, 60″ x 24″ . . . 62 00

Furnishings—See subsequent pages.

Brass Work—n. p. indicates nickel-plated brass work.

For separate illustrations of baths, lavatories and closets, see subsequent pages.

For classification of imperial ware, see page 37.

Plate 1124-A, Bathroom "Nouveau"

THE cost of high-class, modern plumbing fixtures such as these, should be considered in connection with the total cost of the building. The actual value that such equipment will add to the total value of the building, to say nothing of added comfort or saving in repairs, is a factor of importance. On this basis of true economy Mott's Imperial and Vitreous Porcelain fixtures deserve first consideration.

Tiling—The walls are tiled 7' up with a 6" white glazed tile, finished at the top with a cap moulding, and near the base at bottom with a 1" tinted ribbon tile. The floor shows a white 2" vitreous unglazed tile.

Price of fixtures in this bathroom ranges from $240.25 to $270.50; for details, see next page.

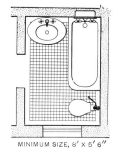

MINIMUM SIZE, 8' X 5' 6"

Plate 1124-A, Bathroom "Nouveau"

	Imp. Porc. Class A	Class B	Vit. Porc.
Bath—The "**Plaza**" imperial porcelain, glazed outside white, with n. p. "**Pembroke**" supply and waste fittings (concealed waste and bell supply, n. p. ¾" compression valves with 4-arm china handles and n. p. escutcheons), 5' x 2' 8" x 17" deep	$154 75	$133 75	
Same, 5' 6" x 2' 8" x 17" deep	175 75	144 25	
Same, 6' x 2' 8" x 17" deep	241 00	193 75	

Note—China escutcheons for "**Pembroke**" bath fittings same price as n. p.

The "**Pembroke**" supply valves are regularly furnished measuring 3" from face of wall to center of valves and are tapped for ¾" i. p. This distance of 3" can be increased at an additional cost.

Note—Traps not included in price of baths; no connections between valves and bell or waste outlet and trap are furnished.

When ordering, state if fittings are to be at right or left end as you face the bath.

	Class A	Class B	Vit. Porc.
Lavatory—The "**Nouveau**" with pedestal, n. p. No. 2 "**Primus**" combination supply and waste with china handles and 1½" n. p. half S trap with i. p. size waste to wall, 27" x 22"	64 00	54 75	$64 00
Same, 32" x 24"	75 50	58 50	75 50
Same, 37" x 27"	86 00	66 50	

Mirror—Beveled oval plate glass with 2⅜" polished wood frame, finished in white enamel, 30" x 22"	20 00	
Same, 33" x 24"	25 25	
Same, 36" x 27"	29 50	

Water Closet—The "**Prompto**" syphon-jet, n. p. No. 2 "**Simplex**" flush and stop valve, No. 6 seat and cover with No. 2 cellu-enamel white finish, n. p. bar hinge and the sanitary-perfect screw connection	51 75	
Same, with cabinet finish quartered oak seat and cover with n. p. bar hinge	46 00	
Imperial porcelain floor slab, extra	3 50	

Furnishings—See subsequent pages.

Brass Work—n. p. indicates nickel-plated brass work.

Tiling—Prices of tiling, set and unset, on application. Diagram of room should accompany inquiry.

For separate illustrations of baths, lavatories and closets, see subsequent pages.

For classification of imperial ware, see page 37.

Plate 1126-A, Bathroom "Vernon"

MODERN plumbing as applied to a bathroom does not consist merely of several appliances that bear no relation one to the other in construction, design or decoration. On the contrary, each element, whether bath, lavatory, water closet or tiling, should be so selected that the bathroom as a whole produces an artistic effect. Plate 1126-A and the other bathrooms in this series, demonstrate what may be accomplished in this line.

Tiling—The walls are 6″ white glazed tile with cap moulding and ½″ tinted ribbon tile forming a light border.

Price of fixtures in this bathroom ranges from $373.00 to $400.25; for details, see next page.

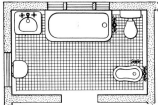

MINIMUM SIZE, 11′ x 6′ 6″

Plate 1126-A, Bathroom "Vernon"

	Imp. Porc. Class A	Class B
Bath—The "Vernon" imperial porcelain, glazed outside white, with n. p. "Unique" supply and waste fittings, 5′ x 2′ 8″ x 17″ deep	$171 50	$148 50
Same, 5′ 6″ x 2′ 8″ x 17″ deep	194 75	160 00
Same, 6′ x 2′ 8″ x 17″ deep	267 25	215 50
If with 4-arm china handles on supply valves, add	2 50	

The "**Unique**" bath fittings are extra heavy and have ¾″ valves and supplies.

Note—When ordering, state if fittings are to be at right or left end as you face the bath.

Lavatory—The "Velasco" vitreous porcelain with vitreous porcelain pedestal, n. p. No. 4 compression "Primus" combination supply and waste (4-arm china handles with china name-plates) and 1½″ n. p. half S trap with i. p. size waste to wall, 27″ x 22″	58 50	
Water Closet—The "Silentis" syphon-jet, seat and cover with No. 1 cellu-enamel white finish, n. p. bar hinge, No. 72 vitreous porcelain cistern with china push-button and the sanitary-perfect screw connection	79 25	
Same, with cabinet finish quartered oak seat and cover with n. p. bar hinge	70 75	
If with "Boston" vent, add	11 75	
If with 2″ right local vent, add	2 25	
Bidet—The "Dunstan" all-porcelain flushing-rim with n. p. combination valves for hot and cold supply to jet and flushing-rim, n. p. rose spray and jet, n. p. "Unique" waste and supply pipes to floor	66 75	
Same, with n. p. combination valves for hot and cold supply to jet and cold supply to flushing-rim	49 75	
Bathroom Seat—Imperial porcelain, with imperial porcelain standard and wall supports	24 25	20 00

While we have reached a point as to quality, in the production of our imperial porcelain ware, beyond anything ever attained heretofore, yet it should be well understood that it is impossible to make large pieces of ware absolutely perfect, i, e., without speck or mark of any kind whatever.

Class A represents the highest average grade of our production. Class B, the second average grade, are also goods of very fine quality and are well suited for high-class work.

The grading of this ware is done with the utmost care by those who understand the business most thoroughly; consequently, unless purchasers select goods from our stock, which is usually a large one, our classification must be accepted. Slight marks or checks in the outside glaze do not affect the classification.

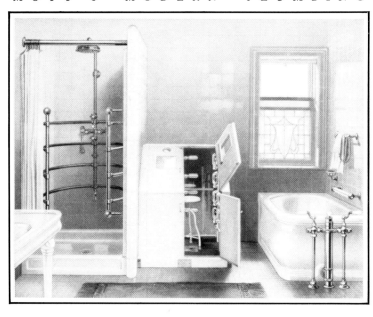

Plate 1128-A, Bathroom "Valando"

THIS is a combination of special fixtures which affords the house owner or physician the benefit of hydrotherapeutic treatment. The electric light cabinet shown above has been approved by the highest authorities. It can be installed in any bathroom wired for ordinary electric current and occupies a space only 43″ by 49″. The combined shower and needle bath is equipped with our special device for indicating and controlling the force and temperature of the water.

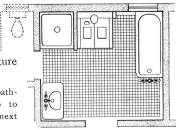

Price of fixtures in this bathroom ranges from $419.50 to $503.25; for details, see next page.

MINIMUM SIZE, 11′ x 9′ 6″

Plate 1128-A, Bathroom "Valando"

	Imp. Porc.	
	Class A	Class B

Bath—The "**La Salle**" imperial porcelain, glazed outside white, with n. p. "**Eton**" supply and waste fittings with china handles, 5′ x 2′ 8″ x 17″ deep . . $152 25 | $120 75

Same, 5′ 6″ x 2′ 8″ x 17″ deep . . . . 162 75 | 131 25

Same, 6′ x 2′ 8″ x 17″ deep . . . . . 214 75 | 167 50

The "**Eton**" fittings are regularly furnished with ¾″ valves and supplies.

If with 1″ valves and supplies and extra large waste, add   21 00

The "**Eton**" bath fittings with the china handles on valves and waste are very handsome. A quarter turn of the handle opens the valves and likewise closes them. For ordinary pressure the Fuller valves are most satisfactory, but for high pressure we advise using the compression, see page 36.

Note—When ordering, state if fittings are to be at right or left end as you face the bath.

Electric Light Cabinet—Price and details on application.

Shower—The "**Regent**" n. p. combination needle and shower bath with 10½″ tubular shower head, n. p. compression valves, check valves, testing valve, lock shield, graduated control valves to wall (one n. p. key included in price of combination), with white duck curtain, curtain rod and snaps, imperial porcelain receptor (39″ x 40″) and n. p. 5″ waste strainer with 3″ coupling . . . . 275 25 | 241 25

If with n. p. "**Thermo**" valve (as Plate 3087½-A, page 89), add 24 00

Lavatory—The "**Valando**" with legs, china wall supports, n. p. compression "**Primus**" combination supply and waste (4-arm china handles with china name-plates) and 1½″ n. p. half S trap with i. p. size waste to wall,

			Vit. Porc.
30″ x 24″	75 75	57 50	$75 75
Same, 33″ x 24″	81 00	61 25	81 00
Same, 36″ x 24″	88 75	67 75	88 75
Same, 42″ x 24″	99 75	80 75	99 75

Mirror—Beveled plate glass with 2⅜″ white enameled wood frame, 30″ x 24″ 23 50

Same, 36″ x 27″ 32 25

Same, 42″ x 30″ 38 00

Brass Work—n. p. indicates nickel-plated brass work.

Tiling—Prices of tiling, set and unset, on application. Diagram of room should accompany inquiry.

For separate illustrations of baths, lavatories and closets, see subsequent pages.

For classification of imperial ware, see page 37.

Plate 1130-A, Bathroom "Pontiac"

THE beauty and substantial character of this bathroom are due to the fact that the fixtures are of Mott's Imperial and Vitreous Porcelain.

The "Pontiac" is a new design bath, glazed inside and outside, which we are enabled to offer at an extremely low price. Its weight is but little more than that of an enameled iron built-in bath.

Tiling—The walls are tiled 7' up with a 6" white glazed tile, finished at the top with a cap moulding, and near the base at bottom with a 1" tinted ribbon tile. The floor shows a white 2" vitreous unglazed tile.

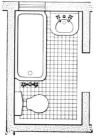

Price of fixtures in this bathroom ranges from $181.00 to $202.00; for details, see next page.

MINIMUM SIZE, 8' X 5' 6"

Plate 1130-A, Bathroom "Pontiac"

	Imp. Porc. Class A	Imp. Porc. Class B
Bath—The "Pontiac" imperial porcelain, glazed outside white, with n. p. "Plymouth" supply and waste fittings, 5' x 2' 6½" x 17" deep	$107 50	$86 50
Same, 5' 6" x 2' 6½" x 17" deep	118 00	97 00
If with 4-arm china handles on supply valves, add	2 50	

The "Plymouth" bath fittings with ¾" valves and supplies, while similar in appearance to the "Unique" fittings, are not so heavy and there are some differences in detail of construction.

Note—When ordering, state if fittings are to be at right or left end as you face the bath.

Lavatory—The "Velasco" vitreous porcelain with vitreous porcelain pedestal, n. p. No. 2 "Nassau" waste, n. p. "Bronx" low-down compression faucets with china name-plates and 1¼" n. p. half S trap with tubing waste to wall, 24" x 20"	38 25	
Same, 27" x 22"	42 25	
If with i. p. size waste to wall, add for 24", $0.55; 27" $0.65.		

Mirror—Plate glass (not beveled) with 1" half-round white enameled wood frame, 24" x 18"	11 25	
Same, 27" x 20"	13 00	

Water Closet—The "Silentum" syphon-jet, No. 6 seat and cover with No. 2 cellu-enamel white finish, n. p. bar hinge, No. 74 vitreous porcelain cistern with china lever handle and No. 8 brass floor flange with four porcelain bolt caps	56 25	
Same, with No. 6 cabinet finish quartered oak seat and cover with n. p. bar hinge	50 50	
Imperial porcelain floor slab, extra	3 50	

Supply pipe, n. p. (i. p. size) to floor with stop valve, less union, extra, $2.00. Same, less stop valve, $1.00.

Furnishings—See subsequent pages.

Brass Work—n. p. indicates nickel-plated brass work.

Tiling—Prices of tiling, set and unset, on application. Diagram of room should accompany inquiry.

For separate illustrations of baths, lavatories and closets, see subsequent pages.

For classification of imperial ware, see page 37.

Plate 1132-A, Bathroom "Pomona"

THE "Pomona" is a new type of inexpensive solid porcelain bath, glazed inside and out; its weight is about the same as that of a built-in enameled iron bath.

The available bath recess will sometimes exceed the length of the bath. By forming a tiled ledge at the foot of bath, with removable white glass or marble top as shown, the fittings are easily accessible; the width of the ledge being varied to fit the bath to the recess.

Price of fixtures in this bathroom ranges from $245.25 to $266.25; for details, see next page.

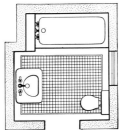

MINIMUM SIZE, 7' 6" x 7'

Plate 1132-A, Bathroom "Pomona"

	Imp. Porc.	
	Class A	Class B

Bath—The "**Pomona**" imperial porcelain, glazed outside white, with n. p. "**Pallas**" supply and waste fittings (concealed waste and bell supply, n. p. ⅝" compression valves with 4-arm china handles and n. p. escutcheons), 5' x 2' 6½" x 17" deep . . . $108 75 / $87 75

Same, 5' 6" x 2' 6½" x 17" deep . . . . 119 25 / 98 25

The "**Pomona**" bath with n. p. "**Ardsley**" fittings (as Plate 2129-A, page 67), same price as above.

Note—China escutcheons for "**Pallas**" bath fittings, extra, $0.75; "**Ardsley**" fittings, $0.50.

For details of "**Pallas**" bath fittings, see page 47.

Note—Traps not included in price of baths; no connections between valves and bell or waste outlet and trap are furnished.

When ordering, state if fittings are to be at right or left end as you face the bath.

Shower—n. p. tubular shower with 8½" tubular shower head, with n. p. combination shower valves, curved curtain rod, white duck curtain, chain and hook . . 45 75

Lavatory—The "**Velasco**" vitreous porcelain with vitreous porcelain pedestal, n. p. No. 4 compression "**Primus**" combination supply and waste (4-arm china handles with china name-plates) and 1½" n. p. half S trap with i. p. size waste to wall, 27" x 22" . . 58 50

If with n. p. 5-ball handles instead of 4-arm china handles, deduct 2 50

Mirror—Plate glass (not beveled) with 1⅝" white enameled wood frame, 27" x 20" 11 25

Water Closet—The "**Beekman**" syphon-jet, No. 6 seat and cover with No. 2 cellu-enamel white finish, n. p. bar hinge, No. 74 vitreous porcelain cistern with china lever handle and No. 8 brass floor flange with four porcelain bolt caps 53 25

Same, with No. 6 cabinet finish quartered oak seat and cover with n. p. bar hinge 47 50

If with "**Boston**" vent, add 11 75

If with 2" right local vent, add 2 25

Imperial porcelain floor slab, extra . . . 3 50

Supply pipe, n. p. (i. p. size) to floor with stop valve, less union, extra, $2.00. Same, less stop valve, $1.00.

Tiling—The walls are of white glazed tile about 4' high, except shower recess which is tiled well up to the curtain ring. The floor is of 1" vitreous tile.

For classification of imperial ware, see page 37.

Plate 1134-A, Bathroom "Altoona"

THIS interior shows the possibility of planning a tiled recess for shower and needle bath within the space afforded by the average sized room. The plate-glass mirror set in the door is an inexpensive convenience too often overlooked in fitting up the bathroom.

Tiling—The walls are of white tile, about 48″ in height with cap moulding and 9″ sanitary base. Back of the shower, the tile should be carried up to a height of 8′ with a width of 3′ on either wall. The floor is of 2″ x 2″ vitreous tile.

Price of fixtures in this bathroom ranges from $182.00 to $200.25; for details, see next page.

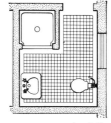

MINIMUM SIZE, 8′ X 6′ 6″

Plate 1134-A, Bathroom "Altoona"

	Imp. Porc.	
	Class A	Class B

Shower—The "Reina" n. p. 10½″ tubular shower, with arm to wall, n. p. "Thermo" improved anti-scalding valve with loose key regulating valves and n. p. handle, n. p. supplies to wall (one n. p. key included in price of combination), imperial porcelain receptor (36″ x 37″), white duck curtain, n. p. curtain rod with wall flanges and curtain snaps, n. p. 5″ waste strainer with 3″ coupling . $116 25 $98 00

Lavatory—The "Altoona" vitreous porcelain with vitreous porcelain standard, china wall supports, n. p. No. 2 "Nassau" waste, n. p. "Excello" low-down compression basin faucets with china name-plates and 1¼″ n. p. half S trap with i. p. size waste to wall, 24″ x 20″ 36 25

Same, 27″ x 22″ 38 50

If with n. p. "Acme" self-closing push-button faucets (as Plate 4326-A, page 78), add 2 25

Mirror—Plate glass (not beveled) with 1″ half-round white enameled wood frame, 24″ x 18″ . . . 11 25

Same, 27″ x 20″ 13 00

Water Closet—The "Beekman" syphon-jet with n. p. No. 2 "Simplex" flush and stop valve, No. 6 seat and cover with No. 2 cellu-enamel white finish, n p. bar hinge and No. 8 brass floor flange with four porcelain bolt caps 47 75

Same, with No. 6 cabinet finish quartered oak seat and cover with n. p. bar hinge 42 00

If with "Boston" vent, add 11 75

Imperial porcelain floor slab, extra . . . 3 50

Furnishings—See subsequent pages.

While we have reached a point as to quality, in the production of our imperial porcelain ware, beyond anything ever attained heretofore, yet it should be well understood that it is impossible to make large pieces of ware absolutely perfect, *i. e.*, without speck or mark of any kind whatever.

Class A represents the highest average grade of our production. Class B, the second average grade, are also goods of very fine quality and are well suited for high-class work.

The grading of this ware is done with the utmost care by those who understand the business most thoroughly; consequently, unless purchasers select goods from our stock, which is usually a large one, our classification must be accepted. Slight marks or checks in the outside glaze do not affect the classification.

For separate illustrations of lavatories and closets, see subsequent pages.

Plate 1136-A, Bathroom "Putnam"

THIS is a good example of a moderate cost bathroom. The "Putnam" is one of the types of our new light weight solid porcelain baths. They are glazed inside and outside and compare favorably in price and weight with the better grade built-in enameled iron baths.

The three porcelain fixtures shown require a minimum space, and can be adapted to any small bathroom.

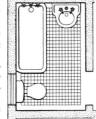

MINIMUM SIZE, 8' X 5' 6"

Tiling—Very simple in character, about 48" high, white tile with cap moulding. Square 2" tile are shown on the floor, a row of darker 2" tile forming a border.

Price of fixtures in this bathroom ranges from $176.75 to $203.75; for details, see next page.

Plate 1136-A, Bathroom "Putnam"

	Imp. Porc. Class A	Class B	
Bath—The "Putnam" imperial porcelain, glazed outside white, n. p. "Pallas" supply and waste fittings (concealed waste and bell supply, n. p. ⅝" compression valves with n. p. escutcheons), 5' x 2' 6½" x 17" deep	$106 25	$85 25	
Same, 5' 6" x 2' 6½" x 17" deep	116 75	95 75	
If with 4-arm china handles on supply valves, add	2 50		

Note—China escutcheons for "Pallas" bath fittings, extra, $0.75.

The "Pallas" supply valves measure 3" from face of wall to center of valves and are tapped for ¾" i. p. In a thicker wall the valves can be partially or entirely buried. The valves, however, cannot be lengthened.

Note—Traps not included in price of baths; no connections between valves and bell or waste outlet and trap are furnished.

When ordering, state if fittings are to be at right or left end as you face the bath.

	Imp. Porc.		Vit. Porc.
Shower—The "Harlem" n. p. shower and shampoo with tubular shower head, curtain ring, white duck curtain, chain and hook, check valves and n. p. supply pipes to wall	20 25		
Lavatory—The "Verona" with standard n. p. No. 2 "Nassau" waste, n. p. "Bronx" low-down compression faucets with china name-plates and 1¼" n. p. half S trap with i. p. size waste to wall, 24" x 22"	35 00	29 00	$37 50
Mirror—Beveled plate-glass oval mirror with 1⅝" wood frame, finished in white enamel, 30" x 22"	20 00		
Water Closet—The "Lombard" syphon-jet, No. 9 seat and cover with No. 2 cellu-enamel white finish, n. p. bar hinge, No. 77 vitreous porcelain cistern with china lever handle and No. 8 brass floor flange with four porcelain bolt caps	42 25		
Same, with No. 9 golden oak or birch-stained mahogany, rubbed seat and cover with n. p. bar hinge	38 00		
If with 2" right local vent, add	2 25		
Imperial porcelain floor slab, extra	3 50		

Supply pipe, n. p. (i. p. size) to floor with stop valve, less union, extra, $2.00. Same, less stop valve, $1.00.

Furnishings—See subsequent pages.

Brass Work—n. p. indicates nickel-plated brass work.

Tiling—Prices of tiling, set and unset, on application. Diagram of room should accompany inquiry.

For separate illustrations of baths, lavatories and closets, see subsequent pages.

For classification of imperial ware, see page 45.

Plate 1138-A, Bathroom "Venetian"

THIS interior illustrates an inexpensive equipment of solid porcelain fixtures. The " Knickerbocker " bath is glazed inside and out, standing free from the wall.

The " Venetian " lavatory with integral shelf can also be furnished with combination valves and spout through the back thus eliminating faucets from the slab and delivering mixed water to the bowl.

Tiling—The room is tiled up to the ceiling—the design is of a delicate empire-colonial character in white or gold and pale green. The floor is 2″ tile.

Price of fixtures in the above interior ranges from $234.25 to $240.25; for details, see next page.

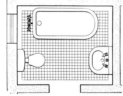

MINIMUM SIZE, 7′ 6″ x 6′

Plate 1138-A, Bathroom "Venetian"

	Imp. Porc. Class A	Porc. Class B
Bath—The **"Knickerbocker"** imperial porcelain, glazed outside white, with n. p. **"Bronx"** combination supply and waste fittings, 4′ 6″ x 2′ 6″ x 17″ deep	$93 00	$87 00
Same, 4′ 10″ x 2′ 6″ x 17″ deep	97 25	90 75
Same, 5′ 4″ x 2′ 6″ x 17″ deep	103 50	96 50
Same, 6′ x 2′ 6″ x 17″ deep	134 25	124 75
If with exterior white enamel paint finish, deduct	12 50	
If with 4-arm china handles on supply valves, add	2 50	

The " Bronx " bath fittings are durable and well made. The supply valves and supply pipes are ½″.

Note—When ordering, state if fittings are to be at right or left end as you face the bath.

Shower—n. p. tubular shower, with 8½″ tubular shower head and rubber-bound shampoo, 25″ curtain ring, white duck curtain, chain and hook and n. p. supply pipes to wall with check valves 45 25

Lavatory—The **"Venetian"** vitreous porcelain with integral back, shelf and wall support, vitreous porcelain standard, n. p. No. 2 "Nassau" waste, n. p. "Bronx" low-down compression faucets with china name-plates and 1½″ n. p. half S trap with i. p. size waste to wall, 24″ x 22″ 44 75

Same, with n. p. "Belknap" ⅝″ combination supply faucet, and n. p. chain stay plug and chain . . 48 50

Mirror—Beveled plate glass with 2⅜″ wood frame, finished white enamel, 30″ x 24″ 15 75

Water Closet—The **"Prompto"** syphon-jet, No. 6 seat and cover with No. 2 cellu-enamel white finish, n. p. bar hinge, No. 74 vitreous porcelain cistern with china lever handle and the sanitary-perfect screw connection 57 25

Same, with No. 6 cabinet finish quartered oak seat and cover with n. p. bar hinge 51 50

Imperial porcelain floor slab, extra . . . 3 50

Supply pipe, n. p. (i. p. size) to floor with stop valve, less union, extra, $2.00. Same, less stop valve, $1.00.

Furnishings—See subsequent pages.

Brass Work—n. p. indicates nickel-plated brass work.

Tiling—Prices of tiling, set and unset, on application. Diagram of room should accompany inquiry.

For separate illustrations of baths, lavatories and closets, see subsequent pages.

For classification of imperial ware, see page 45.

Plate 1140-A, Bathroom "Universo"

A SOLID imperial porcelain bath is the best and most desirable in every respect. The "Universo" costs and weighs about the same as a high-grade enameled iron bath, while the expense of handling and installation is no greater.

Tiling—This may be as shown in any of the following illustrations, and 42″ or 48″ high.

Price of fixtures in this bathroom ranges from $154.50 to $159.50; for details, see next page.

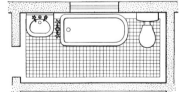

MINIMUM SIZE, 11′ x 5′ 6″

Plate 1140-A, Bathroom "Universo"

	Imp. Porc. Class A	Class B
Bath—The "Universo" imperial porcelain, glazed outside white, with n. p. "Bronx" combination supply and waste fittings and glazed porcelain feet, 4′ 6″ x 2′ 6″ x 17″ deep	$84 75	$79 75
Same, 4′ 10″ x 2′ 6″ x 17″ deep	89 25	83 75
Same, 5′ 4″ x 2′ 6″ x 17″ deep	96 00	89 75
If with exterior white enamel paint finish, deduct	12 50	
If with 4-arm china handles on supply valves, add	2 50	

The "Bronx" bath fittings are durable and well made. The supply valves and supply pipes are ½″.

Note—The height of bath on legs is 23½″; width of roll rim, 3″.

When ordering, state if fittings are to be at right or left end as you face the bath.

Lavatory—The "Veritas" vitreous porcelain with integral back and wall support, vitreous porcelain standard, n. p. No. 2 "Unique" waste, n. p. "Bronx" low-down compression faucets with china name-plates and 1¼″ n. p. half S trap with i. p. size waste to wall, 24″ x 19″		32 50
Same, 27″ x 22″		37 50
Same, 27″ x 22″ with n. p. No. 4 compression "Primus" combination supply and waste (4-arm china handles), as Plate 1132-A		50 75
Mirror—Beveled plate-glass with 1⅝″ white enameled wood frame, 24″ x 18″		11 00
Same, 27″ x 20″		12 50
Water Closet—The "Lombard" syphon-jet, No. 9 seat and cover with No. 2 cellu-enamel white finish, n. p. bar hinge, No. 74 vitreous porcelain cistern with china lever handle and No. 8 brass floor flange with four porcelain bolt caps		42 25
Same, with No. 9 golden oak or birch-stained mahogany, rubbed seat and cover, with n. p. bar hinge		38 00
If with 2″ right local vent, add		2 25
Imperial porcelain floor slab, extra		3 50

Supply pipe, n. p. (i. p. size) to floor with stop valve, less union, extra, $2.00. Same, less stop valve, $1.00.

Furnishings—See subsequent pages.

Brass Work—n. p. indicates nickel-plated brass work.

For separate illustrations of baths, lavatories and closets, see subsequent pages.

For classification of imperial ware, see page 45.

Plate 1142-A, Bathroom "Elsmere"

MOTT'S fixtures represent the last development of sanitary science—as well as the most modern examples of design and workmanship.

With the "Elsmere" bath, as shown above, the enameled cast-iron front plate is carried around beyond the corner, the joint between the front and end piece being at the end. This arrangement gives an unbroken front to the bath, which is impossible with the ordinary bath of this type having the joint between the front and end plate at the corner.

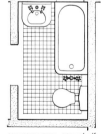

Tiling—The wall tiling is plain white, about 48″ high. It is relieved by a 1″ tinted ribbon tile near the base and two similar ½″ tinted tiles near the top, making a border. The floor is of square 4″ glazed or unglazed vitreous tile.

Fixtures in this bathroom list at $171.70; for details, see next page.

MINIMUM SIZE, 8′ X 5′ 6″

Plate 1142-A, Bathroom "Elsmere"

Bath—The "Elsmere" enameled iron, with enameled iron front and end, n. p. "Unique" supply and waste fittings, 5′ 2″ $100 00

Same, 5′ 8″ 106 00

If exterior is painted one coat, deduct for all sizes . 15 75

If exterior is white enameled painted, deduct for all sizes 4 75

The "**Unique**" bath fittings are extra heavy and have ¾″ valves and supplies.

Note—When ordering, state if fittings are to be at right or left end as you face the bath.

Lavatory—The "Veritas" vitreous porcelain with integral back and wall support, vitreous porcelain standard, n. p. No. 2 "Nassau" waste, n. p. "Bronx" low-down compression faucets with china name-plates and 1¼″ n. p. half S trap with tubing waste to wall, 24″ x 19″ 29 45

Same, 27″ x 22″ 34 45

If traps are furnished with i. p. size waste to wall, add for 24″, $0.55; 27″, $0.65.

Mirror—Plain plate glass with 1⅝″ wood frame, white enameled finish, 24″ x 18″ 10 00

Same, 27″ x 20″ 11 25

Water Closet—The "Lombard" syphon-jet, No. 9 seat and cover with No. 2 cellu-enamel white finish, n. p. bar hinge, No. 74 vitreous porcelain cistern with china lever handle and No. 8 brass floor flange with four porcelain bolt caps 42 25

Same, with No. 9 golden oak or birch-stained mahogany, rubbed seat and cover with n. p. bar hinge . . 38 00

If with 2″ right local vent, add 2 25

Imperial porcelain floor slab, extra 3 50

Supply pipe, n. p. (i. p. size) to floor with stop valve, less union, extra, $2.00. Same, less stop valve, $1.00.

Furnishings—See subsequent pages.

Brass Work—n. p. indicates nickel-plated brass work.

Tiling—Prices of tiling, set and unset, on application. Diagram of room should accompany inquiry.

For separate illustrations of baths, lavatories and closets, see subsequent pages.

Plate 1144-A, Bathroom "Everett"

THE interesting feature of this interior is the enameled iron bath, tiled into the floor and walls, leaving only the interior and enameled front to be kept clean. Such an arrangement is of value in rooms of limited size where the cost contemplated does not permit the use of the solid porcelain bath.

Tiling — This may be as shown in any of the following illustrations, and 42″ or 48″ high.

Fixtures in this bathroom list at $150.25; for details, see next page.

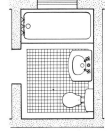

MINIMUM SIZE, 7′ 6″ X 5′ 6″

Plate 1144-A, Bathroom "Everett"

Bath—The "Everett" enameled iron, painted one coat outside, with n. p. "Pallas" supply and waste fittings (concealed waste and bell supply, n. p. ⅝″ compression valves with n. p. escutcheons), 5′ $64 50

Same, 5′ 6″ 69 50

If with 4-arm china handles on supply valves, add . 2 50

Note—China escutcheons for "Pallas" bath fittings, extra, $0.75.

If exterior is white enameled painted, add for all sizes 8 50

If exterior is porcelain enameled, add for all sizes 12 00

For details of "Pallas" bath fittings, see page 47.

Note — Traps not included in price of baths; no connections between valves and bell or waste outlet and trap are furnished.

When ordering, state if fittings are to be at right or left end as you face the bath.

Dimensions—Lengths over all, 5′½″ and 5′ 6½″; outside width, 2′ 5¾″; inside, 2′ ¾″; height on base, 1′ 6¼″; inside depth, 1′ 5″; width of roll-rim, 3″; rim at back and wall ends, 2″.

Lavatory—The "Varian" vitreous porcelain (no back), with vitreous porcelain standard, china wall supports, n. p. "Trinity" waste, n. p. "Bronx" low-down compression faucets with china name-plates and 1½″ n. p. half S trap with i. p. size waste to wall, 24″ x 21″ . 32 50

The "Vermilye" vitreous porcelain with integral back and wall support, screws and washers, vitreous porcelain standard, n. p. "Trinity" waste, n. p. "Bronx" low-down compression faucets with china name-plates, and 1½″ n. p. half S trap with i. p. size waste to wall, 24″ x 21″ 36 25

If with n. p. chain stay, plug and chain, deduct . 3 20

Mirror—Beveled plate glass with white enameled 2⅜″ wood frame, 30″ x 24″ 23 50

Water Closet—The "Beekman" syphon-jet, No. 6 seat and cover with No. 2 cellu-enamel white finish, n. p. bar hinge, No. 74 vitreous porcelain cistern with china lever handle and No. 8 brass floor flange with four porcelain bolt caps 53 25

Same, with No. 6 cabinet finish quartered oak seat and cover with n. p. bar hinge 47 50

If with "Boston" vent, add 11 75

If with 2″ right local vent, add 2 25

Supply pipe, n. p. (i. p. size) to floor with stop valve, less union, extra, $2.00. Same, less stop valve, $1.00.

For separate illustrations of baths, lavatories and closets, see subsequent pages.

Plate 1146-A, Bathroom "Euclid"

THIS interior demonstrates what can be accomplished by the combination of enameled iron and solid porcelain fixtures, when conditions do not warrant the use of the solid porcelain bath.

The "Euclid" is a new design one piece built-in enameled iron bath, which may be furnished with painted or enameled exterior.

Tiling—Plain glazed white about 7' 6" high, relieved with 1" tinted ribbon. The floor may be of 3" square glazed or unglazed vitreous tile with 1" cap moulding.

Fixtures in this bathroom list at $241.00; for details, see next page.

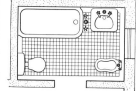

MINIMUM SIZE, 8' 6" x 5' 6"

Plate 1146-A, Bathroom "Euclid"

Bath—The "Euclid" enameled iron, painted one coat outside, with n. p. "Bronx" combination supply and waste fittings, 5' $58 50

Same, 5' 6" 63 50

If with 4-arm china handles on supply valves, add . 2 50

Bath—The "Euclid" as above, with heavy n. p. "Economic" compression faucet with stuffing box, heavy n. p. "Economic" 1½" connected waste and overflow, chain and rubber stopper, and ½" (i. p. size) supply pipes, 5' 53 25

Same, 5' 6" 58 25

If exterior is white enameled painted, add for all sizes . 10 75

If exterior is porcelain enameled, add for all sizes . 15 75

Dimensions—See page 55.

The "Bronx" bath fittings are durable and well made. The supply valves and supply pipes are ½".

Note—When ordering, state if fittings are to be at right or left end as you face the bath.

Shower—n. p. tubular shower with 8½" tubular shower head, with n. p. combination shower valves, curved curtain rod, white duck curtain, chain and hook . . 45 75

Lavatory—The "Ventura" vitreous porcelain with vitreous porcelain pedestal, n. p. chain stay, plug and chain, n. p. "Bronx" low-down compression faucets with china name-plates, and 1¼" n. p. half S trap with tubing waste to wall, 24" x 20" 35 00

Same, 27" x 22" 39 00

If with i. p. size waste add for 24", $0.55; 27", $0.65.

Mirror—Plate glass (not beveled) with 1⅝" white enameled wood frame, 24" x 18" 10 00

Same, 27" x 20" 11 25

Water Closet—The "Beekman" syphon-jet, No. 6 seat and cover with No. 2 cellu-enamel white finish, n. p. bar hinge, No. 74 vitreous porcelain cistern with china lever handle and No. 8 brass floor flange with four porcelain bolt caps 53 25

Same, with No. 6 cabinet finish quartered oak seat and cover with n. p. bar hinge 47 50

If with "Boston" vent, add 11 75

If with 2" right local vent, add 2 25

Bidet—The "Durward" all-porcelain flushing-rim bidet with n. p. combination hot and cold mixing valve to bidet and flushing-rim and n. p. "Nassau" waste . 48 50

Imperial porcelain floor slab, extra 3 50

For separate illustrations of baths, lavatories, closets, and bidets, see subsequent pages.

Plate 1148-A, Bathroom "Emerson"

EXTRA bathrooms for guests and servants are being required in dwellings of even moderate price. In addition to the ever-present convenience to family and guests they add materially to the sales value of the property. The room suggested above is appropriate for guest's bath, or for apartment and hotel equipment. The bath is of high-grade enameled iron, enameled both inside and out. The lavatory is designed to economize space.

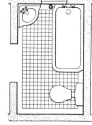

Tiling—The walls are tiled with a 6″ white tile, finished at the top with a plain cap. The floor is of white 2″ vitreous tile.

Price of fixtures in this bathroom ranges from $136.25 to $142.25; for details, see next page.

MINIMUM SIZE, 8′ x 4′ 6″

Plate 1148-A, Bathroom "Emerson"

Bath—The "Emerson" enameled iron, painted one coat outside, with n. p. "Ardsley" fittings, (standing waste through floor with brace to wall, n. p. bell supply and n. p. ⅝″ compression valves in wall with n. p. escutcheons), 5′ $64 50

Same, 5′ 6″ 69 50

If with 4-arm china handles on supply valves, add . 2 50

Note—China escutcheons for "Ardsley" bath fittings, extra, $0.50.

If exterior is white enameled painted, add for all sizes 10 75

If exterior is porcelain enameled, add for all sizes 15 75

Dimensions—See page 55.

The "Ardsley" supply valves measure 3″ from face of wall to center of valves and are tapped for ¾″ i. p. In a thicker wall the valves can be partially or entirely buried. The valves however, cannot be lengthened.

Note—Traps not included in price of baths; no connections between valves and bell or waste outlet and trap are furnished.

When ordering, state if fittings are to be at right or left end as you face the bath.

	Imp. Porc. Class A	Imp. Porc. Class B	Vit. Porc.
Lavatory—The "Vermont", corner, with integral back, standard and painted iron wall supports, n. p chain stay, plug and chain, n. p. "Bronx" low-down compression faucets with china name-plates and 1½″ n. p. half S trap with i. p. size waste to wall, 19″	$35 50	$29 50	$40 25
The "Vassar", vitreous porcelain, corner, with integral back (no standard), n. p. chain stay, plug and chain, n. p. "Bronx" low-down compression faucets with china name-plates and 1¼ n. p. half S trap with tubing waste to wall, 16½″		22 00	
If with n. p. No. 2 "Nassau" waste, add		1 95	

Water Closet—The "Lombard" syphon-jet, No. 9 seat and cover with No. 2 cellu-enamel white finish, n. p. bar hinge, No. 77 vitreous porcelain cistern with china lever handle and No. 8 brass floor flange with four porcelain bolt caps 42 25

Same, with No. 9 golden oak or birch-stained mahogany rubbed seat and cover with n. p. bar hinge . . . 38 00

If with 2″ right local vent, add 2 25

Imperial porcelain floor slab, extra 3 50

Furnishings—See subsequent pages.

Brass Work—n. p. indicates nickel-plated brass work.

For separate illustrations of baths, lavatories and closets see subsequent pages.

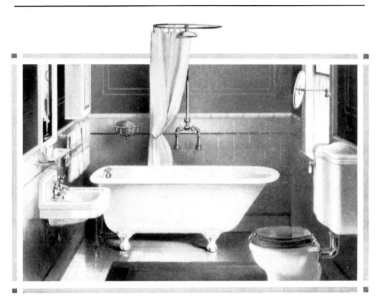

Plate 1150-A, Bathroom "Lombard"

A GROUP of inexpensive fixtures adapted for small bathrooms and apartment houses. At the price of this equipment there is no reason for inadequate number of bathrooms in the modern house.

Tiling—The wall tiling is plain white, about 48" high, with a plain cap moulding. It is relieved by a ½" tinted ribbon tile near the top and a 1" similar tile near the base. The floor is of 4" tile.

Fixtures in this bathroom list at $99.25; for details, see next page.

MINIMUM SIZE, 7' x 5' 6"

Plate 1150-A, Bathroom "Lombard"

Bath—The "Layton" enameled iron, painted one coat outside, with heavy n. p. "Economic" compression faucet, with stuffing box and heavy n. p. "Economic" 1½" connected waste and overflow and ½" (i. p. size) supply pipes; 4', 4' 6" and 5' x 2' 6" x 17" deep . . $32 00

Same, 5' 6" x 2' 6" x 17" deep 35 00

Same, 6' x 2' 6" x 17" deep 41 00

If exterior is white enamel painted on front and ends, add for all sizes 10 25

The "Economic" faucet and "Economic" connected waste and overflow are heavy, well made, first class throughout and guaranteed. We also furnish the "Harlem" competition faucet and "Harlem" 1⅜" connected waste and overflow, lighter in weight (see page 63). We strongly recommend the "Economic" faucet and connected waste and overflow.

Note—When ordering, state if fittings are to be at right or left end as you face the bath.

Shower—The "Harlem" n. p. brass shower with tubular shower head, curtain ring, white duck curtain, check valves and n. p. supply pipes to wall with escutcheons . 13 25

Lavatory—The "Veritas" vitreous porcelain with integral back and wall support, patent overflow, n. p. chain stay, plug and chain, bolts and washers with china caps, n. p. "Bronx" low-down compression faucets with china name-plates and 1¼" n. p. half S trap with tubing waste to wall, 20" x 18" 16 00

Same, 20" x 19", with n. p. No. 2 "Nassau" waste . 19 45

Same, 24" x 19", with n. p. No. 2 "Unique" waste . 26 75

If traps are furnished with i. p. size waste to wall, add 0 55

Mirror—Plain plate glass with 1⅝" wood frame, white enameled finish, 24" x 18" 10 00

Same, 27" x 20" 11 25

Water Closet—The "Lombard" syphon-jet, No. 9 golden oak or birch-stained mahogany, rubbed seat and cover with n. p. bar hinge, No. 77 vitreous porcelain cistern with china lever handle and No. 8 brass floor flange with four porcelain bolt caps . . . 38 00

Same, with No. 9 seat and cover with No. 2 cellu-enamel white finish and n. p. bar hinge 42 25

Imperial porcelain floor slab, extra 3 50

Supply pipe, n. p. (i. p. size) to floor with stop valve, less union, extra, $2.00. Same, less stop valve, $1.00.

For separate illustrations of baths, lavatories and closets, see subsequent pages.

Plate 1152-A, Bathroom "Economic"

THIS is another room of low cost and unusual value. Mott's enameled iron fixtures are designed with the same care as the higher priced goods and are guaranteed to give satisfactory service. The faucets, traps, valves and other metal parts are superior to ordinary goods of their class.

Tiling—The wall tiling is plain white, about 48″ high, with a plain cap moulding. It is relieved by a ½″ tinted ribbon tile near the top and a 1″ similar tile near the floor. The floor is of 4″ tile.

Fixtures in this bathroom list at $92.75; for details, see next page.

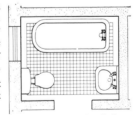

MINIMUM SIZE, 7′ X 5′ 6″

Plate 1152-A, Bathroom "Economic"

Bath—The "Layton" enameled iron, painted one coat outside, with n. p. "Harlem" compression faucet, n. p. "Harlem" 1⅜″ connected waste and overflow, chain and rubber stopper and ½″ (i. p. size) supply pipes; 4′, 4′ 6″ and 5′ x 2′ 6″ x 17″ deep $30 25

Same, 5′ 6″ x 2′ 6″ x 17″ deep 33 25

Same, 6′ x 2′ 6″ x 17″ deep 39 25

If exterior is white enamel painted on front and ends, add for all sizes 10 25

For price of "Layton" bath with heavy "Economic" fittings, see page 61.

Note—When ordering, state if fittings are to be at right or left end as you face the bath.

Shower—The "Harlem" n. p. brass shower and shampoo with tubular shower, curtain ring, white duck curtain, check valves and n. p. supply pipes to wall with escutcheons 20 25

Lavatory—The "Bromley" enameled iron, with patent overflow, back and apron, n. p. plug and chain, n. p. "Harlem" low-down compression faucets with china name-plates, and 1¼″ n. p. half S trap with tubing waste to wall and "Simplex" hanger, 24″ x 18″ . 15 00

Same, 27″ x 22″ 20 25

Soap dish, extra 0 20

If traps are furnished with i. p. size waste to wall, add for 24″, $0.50; 27″, $0.70.

Mirror—Plate glass (not beveled), with 1⅝″ white enameled wood frame, 24″ x 18″ 10 00

Same, 27″ x 20″ 11 25

Water Closet—The "Lawrence" wash-down syphon, No. 9 golden oak or birch-stained mahogany, rubbed seat and cover with n. p. bar hinge, No. 76 vitreous porcelain cistern with china lever handle and No. 8 brass floor flange with four porcelain bolt caps . . . 27 25

Same, with No. 9 seat and cover with No. 2 cellu-enamel white finish and n. p. bar hinge 31 50

If with 2″ right local vent, add 2 25

Imperial porcelain floor slab, extra 3 50

Supply pipe, n. p. (i. p. size) to floor with stop valve, less union, extra, $2.00. Same, less stop valve, $1.00.

Furnishings—See subsequent pages.

Brass Work—n. p. indicates nickel-plated brass work.

Tiling—Prices of tiling, set and unset, on application. Diagram of room should accompany inquiry.

For separate illustrations of baths, lavatories and closets, see subsequent pages.

Plate 2016½-A. "La Salle" imperial porcelain bath, glazed outside white, with n. p. "Unique" supply and waste fittings (compression valves)

Plate 2013-A. "Baronial" bath with n. p. "Eton" fittings (Fuller valves), see page 24

For description and prices of "La Salle" bath, see pages 19 and 39; "Baronial", see page 25.

Plate 2028-A. "Plaza" imperial porcelain bath, glazed outside white, with "Pembroke" supply and waste fittings

Plate 2026-A. "Pierpont" bath with n. p. "Penroy" fittings, see page 26

For description and prices of "Plaza" bath, see pages 13, 29 and 35; "Pierpont", see page 27.

Plate 2118-A. "Empress" imperial porcelain bath, glazed outside white, with n. p. "Pallas" supply and waste fittings

Plate 2123-A. "Prescott" bath with n. p. "Pembroke" supply and waste fittings

For description and prices of "Empress" bath, see pages 17 and 31; "Prescott", see page 15.

Plate 2117-A. The "Vernon" imperial porcelain bath, glazed outside white, with n. p. "Unique" supply and waste fittings (compression valves)

Plate 2124-A. "Vernon" bath with n. p. "Eton" fittings (Fuller valves), see page 20

For description and prices of "Vernon" bath, see pages 21 and 37.

Plate 2125-A. The "**Pontiac**" imperial porcelain bath, glazed outside white, with n. p. "**Plymouth**" supply and waste fittings with 4-arm china handles

For description and prices of "**Pontiac**" bath, see page 41.

The "**Pontiac**", "**Pomona**" and "**Putnam**" are our latest types of light weight solid porcelain baths with straight ends. In weight and price they compare favorably with the better grade of built-in enameled iron baths.

A great forward step in the pottery art is represented by these baths. The "**Pontiac**", "**Putnam**" and "**Pomona**" mark an epoch in the production of solid porcelain baths for the reason that they meet two factors which in many classes of work are of prime importance, namely, reduction in weight and price.

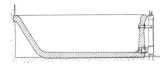 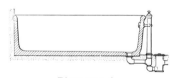

Plate 2132-A

Longitudinal section of the "La Salle" and "Baronial" solid imperial porcelain baths

Plate 2131-A

Longitudinal section of the "Pontiac" solid imperial porcelain bath

Plate 2129-A. The "**Pomona**" imperial porcelain bath, glazed outside white, with n. p. "**Ardsley**" fittings

For description and prices of "**Pomona**" bath, see page 43.

Plate 2127-A. The "**Putnam**" imperial porcelain bath, glazed outside white, with n. p. "**Pallas**" supply and waste fittings

For description and prices of "**Putnam**" bath, see page 47.

Plate 2088½-A

Plate 2088½ A. The "Knickerbocker" imperial porcelain bath, glazed outside white, with n. p. "Bronx" supply and waste fittings

For description and prices of "Knickerbocker" bath, see page 49

Plate 2040-A

Plate 2040-A. The "Grantham" imperial porcelain bath, glazed outside white, with n. p. "Eton" supply and waste fittings with china handles

For description and prices of "Grantham" bath, see page 23

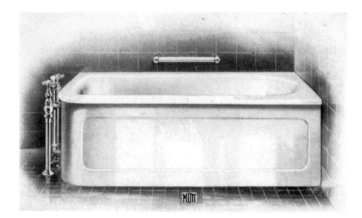

Plate 2750-A

Plate 2750-A. The "Elsmere" enameled iron bath with enameled iron front and end, n. p. "Unique" supply and waste fittings, 5' 2" . . $100 00
Same, 5' 8" 106 00
If with 4-arm china handles on supply valves, add 2 50

Plate 2751-A. The "Elsmere" as above, with n. p. "Eton" supply and waste fittings with china handles (as Plate 2755-A), 5' 2" . . 105 50
Same, 5' 8" 111 50
If exterior is painted one coat, deduct for all sizes . . . 15 75
If exterior is white enamel painted, deduct for all sizes . . . 4 75

With the "Elsmere" and "Egmont" baths the enameled cast-iron front plate is carried around beyond the corner, the joint between the front and end piece being at the end. This arrangement gives an unbroken front to the bath which is impossible with the ordinary type of bath having the joint between the front and end plate at the corner.

The "Eton" fittings with the china handles on valves and waste are very handsome. A quarter turn of the handle opens the valves and likewise closes them. For ordinary pressure the Fuller valves are most satisfactory, but for high pressure we advise using the compression, as Plate 2750-A.

Note—When ordering, state if fittings are to be at right or left end as you face the bath.

For dimensions and section of "Elsmere" bath, see page 70.

Plate 2755-A

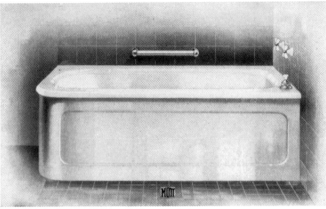

Plate 2756-A

Plate 2756-A. The "**Egmont**" enameled iron bath with enameled iron front and end, n. p. "**Eclipse**" supply and waste fittings (standing waste through rim and n.p. bell supply, ⅝" compression valves with 4-arm china handles and china escutcheons), 5′ 2″ $101 00
Same, 5′ 8″ 107 00

Plate 2757-A. The "**Egmont**" as above, with n. p. "**Pallas**" supply and waste fittings (concealed waste and bell supply, n. p. ⅝" compression valves with n. p. escutcheons), 5′ 2″ 99 00
Same, 5′ 8″ 105 00
If exterior is painted one coat, deduct for all sizes . . . 15 75
If exterior is white enamel painted, deduct for all sizes . 4 75

Dimensions—Lengths over all, 5′ 2½″ and 5′ 8½″; outside width, 2′ 8″; inside, 2′ 1½″; height, 1′ 10¾″; inside depth, 1′ 6″; width of rim, front, 3½″; back, 3″; wall end, 4″.

The "**Eclipse**" supply valves measure 3″ from face of wall to center of valves and are tapped for ¾″ i. p. In a thicker wall the valves can be partially or entirely buried. The valves, however, cannot be lengthened.

Note—Traps not included in price of baths; no connections between valves and bell or waste outlet and trap, are furnished.

When ordering, state if fittings are to be at right or left end as you face the bath.

Note—The "**Elsmere**", "**Egmont**", "**Elberon**" and "**Exeter**" baths are regularly furnished with iron legs.

Plate 2761-A

Cross section of "Elsmere", "Egmont" and "Elberon" enameled iron baths set in tile walls and floor—showing how separate enameled cast-iron plates are used to enclose the baths.

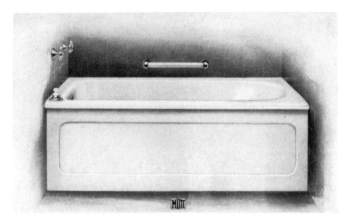

Plate 2758-A

Plate 2758-A. The "**Elberon**" enameled iron bath with enameled iron front, n. p. "**Eclipse**" supply and waste fittings (standing waste through rim and n.p. bell supply, n. p. ⅝" compression valves with n. p. escutcheons), 5′ 2″ . $89 50
Same, 5′ 7″ 95 50
If with 4-arm china handles and china escutcheons on supply valves, add 3 00
If exterior is painted one coat, deduct for all sizes . . . 12 00
If exterior is white enamel painted, deduct for all sizes . . 3 50

Dimensions—Lengths over all, 5′ 2½″ and 5′ 7½″; outside width, 2′ 5½″; inside, 2′ ½″; height, 1′ 10¾″; inside depth, 1′ 6″; width of rim, front, 3″; back, 2″; wall ends, 3″.

For cross section, see page 70.

Plate 2774-A. The "**Exeter**" enameled iron bath, painted one coat outside, with heavy n. p. "**Economic**" compression faucet, with stuffing box and heavy "**Economic**" 1½″ connected waste and overflow and ½″ i. p. size supply pipes, 5′ 2″ $62 50
Same, 5′ 7″ 67 50

The "**Exeter**" bath is intended to be installed with cement or tile front as shown.

Plate 2774-A

Note—When ordering, state if fittings are to be at right or left end as you face the bath.

Plate 2701-A. The "**Euclid**" enameled iron bath, with n. p. "**Bronx**" supply and waste fittings

For description and prices of "Euclid" bath, see page 57.

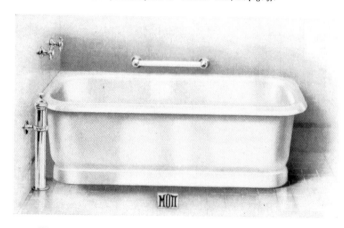

Plate 2703-A. The "**Emerson**" enameled iron bath, with n. p. "**Ardsley**" fittings

The "**Emerson**" bath can also be furnished with "**Pallas**" fittings, as Plate 2704-A

For description and prices of "Emerson" bath, see page 59.

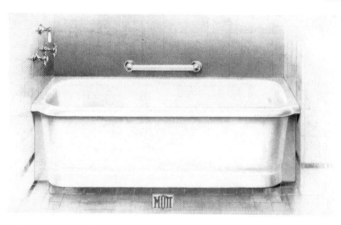

Plate 2704-A. The "**Everett**" enameled iron bath, with n. p. "**Pallas**" supply and waste fittings

For description and prices of "Everett" bath, see page 55.

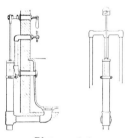

Plate 2556-A

Plate 2760-A

The "**Pallas**" and "**Ardsley**" supply valves measure 3″ from face of wall to center of valves and are tapped for ¾″ i. p. In a thicker wall the valves can be partially or entirely buried. The valves, however, cannot be lengthened.

Note—Traps not included in price of baths; no connections between valves and bell or waste outlet and trap are furnished.

Cross section of "Euclid", "Everett" and "Emerson" enameled iron baths (cast in one piece) set in tile walls and floor.

The outside may be enameled or painted.

The "**Everett**" is adapted for recess where pipe shaft is provided for fittings. If there is no shaft, fittings can be furnished as shown with "**Emerson**" bath.

When ordering, state if fittings are to be at right or left end as you face the bath.

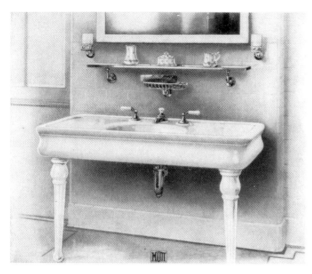

Plate 4013-A

Plate 4013-A. The "Marsden" imperial porcelain lavatory with imperial porcelain legs, china wall supports, n. p. No. 3 "Primus" combination supply and waste with china handles, and 1½" n. p. half S trap with i. p. size waste to wall, 4′ 2″ x 2′ 1″; basin, 18″ x 13″ . . . . . . $128 25 . . $99 25

	Imp. Porc.	
	Class A	Class B
	$128 25	$99 25

Plate 4766-A

Plate 4766-A. Supply pipe to floor, n. p., ⅜″ i. p. size with ¼″ coupling and escutcheon, per pair $2 50

Same, with stop valve, per pair 5 00

If with unions, add extra, per pair 1 25

Plate 4807-A Supply pipe to wall, n. p., ⅜″ i. p. size with stop valve, stuffing box, and escutcheon with reducer tapped for ¼″ i. p., per pair 4 50

Same, less stop valve, per pair . . . 2 50

If with ½″ nipple to wall, instead of ⅜″, add extra, per pair 0 35

Plate 4807-A

74

Plate 4001-A

Plate 4001-A. The "Granville" imperial porcelain lavatory with imperial porcelain legs and china wall supports, n. p. No. 3 "Primus" supplies and wastes with china handles and 1½″ n. p. half S traps with i. p. size wastes to wall . . . $158 75 $127 75

	Imp. Porc.	
	Class A	Class B
	$158 75	$127 75

If with n. p. "Excello" low-down compression faucets with china name-plates and n. p. "Unique" wastes, deduct . . 18 50

If with n. p. shampoo faucet, as Plate 4005-A, add . . 9 00

Dimensions—Length, 4′ 6″; width, 2′ 2″; basins, 19½″ x 14½″.

Mirror—Plate glass with 3¼″ white enameled wood frame, 4′ 10″ x 2′ 6″ 49 25

Same, beveled mirror 53 00

Furnishings—China soap dish with n. p. holder . $3 20

Plate glass shelf, 54″ x 5″ with n. p. brackets . 14 00

China tooth brush vase 45

China mug 60

Cut glass tumbler 75

For prices of other furnishings, see subsequent pages.

In modern residences the tendency is towards larger bathrooms. This is most desirable in every way. Among other advantages, it permits the installation of large and commodious lavatories such as the "Marsden" and "Granville".

Plate 4005-A

75

63

Plate 4391-A. The "Valcour" imperial and vitreous porcelain pedestal lavatory.
For description and prices of "Valcour" lavatory, see pages 13, 15, 23 and 31

Plate 4024-A. The "Norwood" imperial and vitreous porcelain pedestal lavatory.
For description and prices of "Norwood" lavatory, see page 33

Plate 4323-A. The "Velasco" vitreous porcelain pedestal lavatory.
For description and prices of "Velasco" lavatory, see pages 37, 41 and 43

Plate 4317-A. The "Ventura" vitreous porcelain pedestal lavatory.
For description and prices of "Ventura" lavatory, see page 57

Plate 4017-A. The "Victorian" imperial and vitreous porcelain pedestal lavatory.
For description and prices of "Victorian" lavatory, see pages 17, 19 and 21

Plate 4018-A. The "Nouveau" imperial and vitreous porcelain pedestal lavatory.
For description and prices of "Nouveau" lavatory, see pages 25 and 35

Plate 4394-A. The "Valando" imperial and vitreous porcelain lavatory.
For description and prices of "Valando" lavatory, see pages 29 and 39

Plate 4304½-A. The "Verona" imperial and vitreous porcelain lavatory; 7″ back.
For description and prices of "Verona" lavatory, see page 47

Plate 4398-A. The "Varian" vitreous porcelain lavatory.

For description and prices of "Varian" lavatory, see page 55

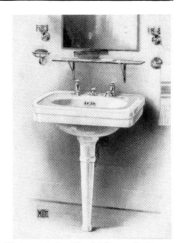

Plate 4326-A. The "Altoona" vitreous porcelain lavatory.

For description and prices of "Altoona" lavatory, see page 45

Plate 4329-A. The "Veritas" vitreous porcelain lavatory.

Height of backs, 6½″ and 8″

For descriptions and prices of "Veritas" lavatory, see pages 51 and 53; "Venetian" lavatory, see page 49

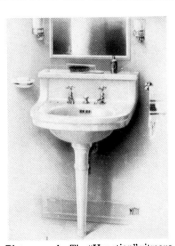

Plate 4375-A. The "Venetian" vitreous porcelain lavatory.

Height of back, 7″

Plate 4311½-A. The "Vermont" imperial and vitreous porcelain corner lavatory.

Projection from corner, 26″; height of back, 5″

For descriptions and prices of "Vermont" and "Vassar" lavatories, see page 59

Plate 4322-A. The "Vassar" vitreous porcelain corner lavatory.

Projection from corner, 22″; height of back, 5″

Plate 4328½-A. The "Veritas" vitreous porcelain lavatory.

Height of backs, 6″ and 6½″

For descriptions and prices of "Veritas" lavatory, see page 61; "Vermilye" lavatory, see page 55

Plate 4397-A. The "Vermilye" vitreous porcelain lavatory.

Height of back, 6½″

Plate 4385-A

Plate 4385-A. The "Vidal" vitreous porcelain lavatory with integral back and wall support, patent overflow, n. p. chain stay, plug and chain, bolts and washers with china caps, n. p. "Bronx" low-down compression faucets with china name-plates and 1¼″ n. p. half S trap with i. p. size waste to wall . . . $22 00

Dimensions—Length, 24″; width, 14″; basin, 16″ x 10″; height of back, 6″.

Plate 4385½-A

Plan view of "Vidal" lavatory showing long bowl, and narrow width. This lavatory is adapted for coat room and under staircase where a lavatory with small projection is desirable.

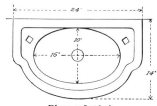

Plate 4385½-A

Plate 4387-A

Plate 4387-A. The "Villar" vitreous porcelain lavatory with integral back and wall support, patent overflow, bolts and washers, with china caps, n. p. "Belknap" ⅝″ combination with 4-arm china handles and china name-plates, n. p. waste strainer, coupling and 1¼″ n. p. half S trap with i. p. size waste to wall . . . $29 50

Dimensions — Length, 17″, width, 14″; basin, 12″ x 10″; height of back, 4″.

Note—No connection between supply valves and nozzle is furnished.

The "Villar" dental lavatory, as shown by Plate 4387-A, is a refinement of bathroom service well worth consideration.

The Sanitary-perfect Screw Connection
(Patented)

IN these days of almost perfection in sanitary science, the connection of the water closet to the soil pipe is the one weak spot in an otherwise admirable system of house plumbing, the one connection that cannot be relied upon under all conditions. Absolute security is assured, and the question of careless or unskilful work disposed of by the sanitary-perfect screw connection; moreover, those who have seen and used this device do not hesitate to say that it solves the question of water closet connection, and recommend the same to their clients as the only perfect connection which they could guarantee under all conditions.

Note—All ordinary connections require bolts through the base of the closet. The sanitary-perfect is a screw connection, hence is absolutely and permanently reliable, and furthermore, it dispenses with unsightly bolts.

Plate 5002½-A shows closet with the sanitary-perfect screw connection and the threaded floor coupling which is connected to soil pipe.

The section of the sanitary-perfect screw connection (Plate 5001-A) shows how the threaded brass screw connection is secured into the base of the closet. The

Plate 5002½-A

joint thus formed makes the brass connection equivalent to an integral part of the closet which is impossible to loosen or disturb in the slightest degree.

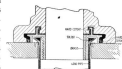

Plate 5001-A

Plate 5569-A. The "Silentis" syphon-jet water closet with cabinet finish quartered oak chair, n. p. wall plate with china lever handle, No. 33 plain pine cistern, japanned brackets, wire pull, brass flush pipe, and the sanitary-perfect screw connection . . . $99 75

Same, with white enameled chair. 111 25

If with n. p. No. 2 "Simplex" flush and stop valve (see Plate 5533-A, page 83), deduct . . . 12 75

To those who prefer a closet chair to the regular form of closet seat, Plate 5569-A will commend itself as the best device of its kind. The flushing device can be placed in an adjoining closet or room, or directly back of the chair.

Plate 5569-A

Plate 5492-A. The "Silentis" syphon-jet water closet with No. 72 vitreous porcelain cistern.

Plate 5485-A. The "Silentis" syphon-jet closet with No. 74 vitreous porcelain cistern.

For description and prices of "Silentis" closet, see pages 15, 17, 19, 23, 25, 31 and 37

Plate 5476-A. The "Lombard" syphon-jet water closet with No. 77 vitreous porcelain cistern.

For description and prices of "Lombard" closet, see pages 47, 51, 53, 59 and 61

Plate 5488-A. The "Lawrence" wash-down syphon water closet with No. 76 vitreous porcelain cistern.

For description and price of "Lawrence" closet, see page 63

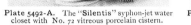

Plate 5471-A. The "Prompto" syphon-jet water closet with No. 74 vitreous porcelain cistern.

For description and prices of "Prompto" closet, see pages 33, 35 and 49

Plate 5475-A. The "Silentum" syphon-jet water closet with No. 74 vitreous porcelain cistern.

For description and price of "Silentum" closet, see page 41

Plate 5533-A. The "Beekman" syphon-jet water closet, with "Boston" vent and No. 2 "Simplex" flush and stop valve.

For description and prices of "Beekman" closet, see pages 43, 45, 55 and 57

Plate 5506-A. The "Langham" syphon-jet water closet with n. p. "Presto" flush valve, adjustable shut-off valve.

For description and prices of "Langham" closet, see pages 13, 21, 27 and 29

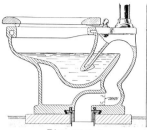

Plate 5641-A

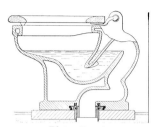

Plate 5652-A

Section of the "Silentis" Syphon Water Closet with Non-soil Flushing-rim, concealed Twin-jet and the Sanitary-perfect Screw Connection

Section of the "Langham" Syphon Water Closet with Non-soil Flushing-rim, Direct-acting concealed jet and the Sanitary-perfect Screw Connection

This closet has an unusually large water area of 13¼" x 10" with depth of seal of 3½".

The "Silentis" is the ideal water closet for the modern residence. By an ingenious arrangement of the supply to the bowl and syphon-jet, the noise of flushing is reduced to a minimum. Running water cannot further be silenced and still produce a sanitary flush.

Other salient features of the "Silentis" are the extra large bowl and seat; concealed jet holes; drain plug which allows removing of water from the bowl without disturbing the soil connection, and the sanitary-perfect screw connection (patented), insuring a permanently tight joint between the closet and soil pipe.

The area of water in bowl is 12" x 10" and the depth of seal is 3½".

Quickness and thoroughness of operation are obtained by the supply to the jet coming from the flush valve in a direct line without loss of power.

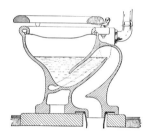

Plate 5674-A

Section of "Lombard" Syphon-jet Water Closet with Non-soil Flushing-rim

The "Lombard" is a small syphon-jet closet and roughs in very close. The length from front to back over all is 20"; height, 15"; area of water in bowl, 10½" x 7"; depth of seal 3". The base is secured to the brass floor flange by 4 bolts, which make a more reliable joint than with only two bolts.

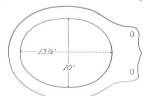

Plate 5642-A

Plan view of the "Silentis" and "Langham" Syphon-jet Water Closets, showing the extra large bowls

---

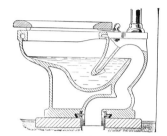

Plate 5647-A

Plate 5643-A

Section of the "Silentis" Syphon Water Closet with "Boston" Vent, Non-soil Flushing-rim and concealed Twin-jet

Section of "Prompto" and "Beekman" Syphon Water Closets with Non-soil Flushing-rim and concealed Twin-jet

Raised "Boston" Vent Water Closets are a Guarantee of a Sanitary Odorless Toilet Room

IN any form of *local ventilation* to be applied to a water closet, the primary object to be obtained is the removal of the foul air in the quickest possible manner. This can best be accomplished by the raised integral vent.

For local ventilation no arrangement yet devised is comparable to the "Boston" vent, shown in Plate 5647-A. In the first place, it is of adequate area; secondly, the construction is such that the vent is above the top edge of the closet, so that any overflow which may take place from stoppage in the closet is not forced into the vent pipe; thirdly, each time the closet is operated the vent pipe is flushed as well as the bowl.

The ordinary closets of this type have the jet pipe on the side, which mars the symmetry and appearance of the closet; moreover, the jet opening in the bottom of the bowl is unsightly and becomes discolored. In the "Prompto" and "Beekman" the jet is concealed from view and so located as to give the maximum efficiency with a limited amount of water (2 to 3 gallons). Quickness and thoroughness of operation are attained by the supply to the jet coming from the flush pipe in a direct line without loss of power. The area of water in bowl is 12" x 10", with a depth of seal of 3¼".

The "Beekman" differs from the "Prompto" only in being secured to the soil pipe by brass flange and bolts, instead of with the sanitary-perfect screw connection.

The "Silentum" is a small syphon-jet water closet with large water area and deep seal. A special feature is its quiet operation.

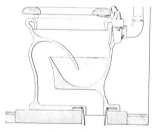

Plate 5649-A

Plate 5649-A. Section of the "Lawrence" wash-down syphon water closet with non-soil flushing-rim.

The "Lawrence" is a combination of the wash-down and syphon types of water closets. The jet strikes directly upon and forces outward the contents of the bowl and causes syphonic action when the closet is operated. The water area is 7" x 8". Where an inexpensive yet good working water closet is required, the "Lawrence" is recommended. The floor flange is secured to the base by four bolts.

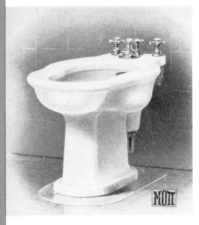

Plate 5925-A. The "Durward" all porcelain flushing-rim bidet.

For description and prices of "Durward" bidet, see pages 23 and 27

Plate 5930-A. The "Duval" all porcelain flushing-rim bidet.

For description and prices of "Duval" bidet, see pages 17 and 19

Plate 5929-A. The "Dunstan" all porcelain flushing-rim bidet.

Plate 5926-A. The "Dunstan" all porcelain flushing-rim bidet.

For description and prices of "Dunstan" bidets, see page 37

86

Plate 3164-A. The "Perry" n. p. combination needle and shower bath.

For description and prices, see page 19

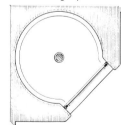

Plate 3164½-A

Dimensions—Diameter of receptor, outside, 42″; width across front, 31″; height from floor to top edge of receptor, about 6½″; depth inside, 5½″; size of door, 5′ 11½″ high and 2′ 3″ wide.

In some bathrooms it is not feasible to use a needle bath with door parallel with either wall. The arrangement shown, Plate 3164-A, may commend itself in such cases, see plan view of receptor, Plate 3164½-A.

Needle and shower baths are coming more and more into favor because of their exhilarating and health-giving properties. In order to produce the proper effect the pressure should be twenty pounds or over at the needle fixture. If lower pressure than this is used, the spray will not have the same stimulating effect.

87

69

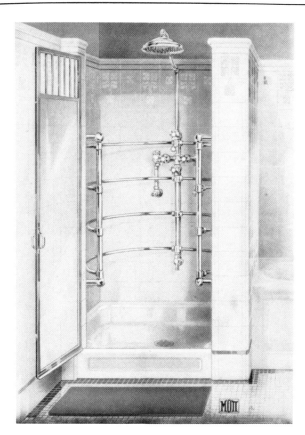

Plate 3161-A

Plate 3161-A. The "Regent" n. p. combination needle and shower bath.

For description and prices, see pages 13, 15 and 17.

Dimensions of Receptor—Outside, from right to left, 39″; front to back, 40″; height, from floor to top edge of receptor, about 8″; depth, inside, 6″; size of door, 5′ 11½″ high and 2′ 3″ wide.

For plan view of receptor, see Plate 3161½-A.

If it is desired to control the hot water so as to minimize the danger of scalding, we know of no better apparatus than the "Lawler" regulator; details on application.

Note—To obtain proper results with the needle baths, the water pressure should be at least twenty pounds and the supply pipes amply large.

"Thermo" Improved Anti-Scalding Valve

Plate 3087½-A

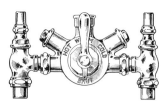

Plate 3088½-A

Plate 3087½-A illustrates the "Thermo" n. p. improved anti-scalding valve with n. p. handle and index ring and pointer.

Plate 3088½-A illustrates the "Thermo" n. p. improved anti-scalding valve with n. p. handle, index ring and pointer, and loose key regulating valves on hot and cold supply.

Special attention is directed to the following improvements in the "Thermo" anti-scalding valve, which makes it the best of its kind on the market:

First—The ball-bearing action between the valve spindle and cam gives an easy movement to the valve.

Second—The valve has an adjustable stop accessible from the outside of casing, by which the hot water may be increased or diminished. In other words, if the valve is delivering hot water at 120 degrees, this stop can be set so as to cut it down to 100 or 105 degrees or to practically whatever degree is desired, provided the conditions do not change.

Third—A frictional member has been introduced between the valve spindle and casing which is sure and simple in operation and does not produce any binding no matter how hot the parts become.

Fourth—The angle graduated control valves for hot and cold supply are so constructed that they give a very fine adjustment as to the amount of hot or cold water that will pass through them. By this means the supply entering at a great difference of temperature and pressure can be regulated to suit any reasonable conditions.

The "Thermo" improved anti-scalding valve with graduated regulating valves has been thoroughly tested under all conditions, such as extreme variations in the temperature of the water supply and difference in pressure of the hot or cold water. These tests have demonstrated that the "Thermo" improved valve can be depended upon to operate satisfactorily.

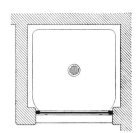

By placing the valves on the side of the stall, the temperature of water can be regulated before going into the enclosure.

The adjustable shower head, as shown in Plate 3167-A, is located slightly above the level of the shoulders and arranged to throw the water diagonally across the shoulders and body, without wetting the hair; price on application.

Plate 3161½-A

Plate 3167-A

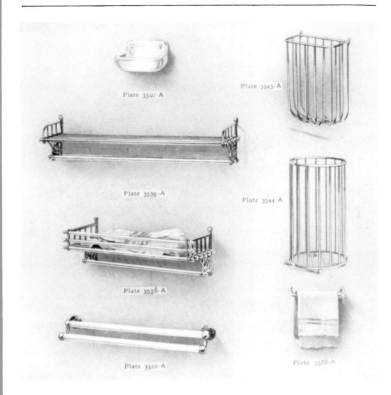

Plate 3536-A. Combination towel shelf
and rack, 20″ long, 6″ wide . . . $4 75
Same, 26″ long, 6″ wide . . . 5 50

Plate 3522-A. Double towel rack, Crystal Opaloid
18″ long $6 00 $6 50
Same, 24″ long . . . 6 50 7 30
Same, 30″ long . . . 7 00 8 10

Plate 3544-A. Basket for soiled towels . 14 00

Plate 3545-A. Basket for soiled towels . 12 75

Plate 3541-A. Porcelain soap dish, 6¼″
x 4″ $1 05

Plate 3538-A. Combination towel shelf
and rack :
Size 1, 20″ long 6 25
Size 2, 26″ long 7 00
Size 3, 30″ long 7 50
The above are 6″ wide.

Plate 3566-A. Hook for towels, 5″ long 0 65

All brass work of furnishings on pages 90 to 97 is nickel-plated. Discount on furnishings, pages 90 to
97, ten per cent.

Plate 3573-A. Holder . . . $1 65
Cut glass tumbler 0 75

Plate 3574-A. Holder, china vase and cut
glass tumbler 4 95

Plate 3578-A. Holder, china dish and vase 4 15

Plate 3571-A. Holder, china dish, vase,
and cut glass tumbler . . . 8 40

Plate 3709-A. Holder . . . 1 50
Cut glass tumbler 0 75

Plate 3710-A. Holder, china dish, vase,
and cut glass tumbler . . . $9 00

Plate 3711-A. Holder with china vase . 2 00

Plate 3712-A. Holder, china dish and vase 6 75

Plate 3713-A. Holder, china vase and cut
glass tumbler 4 10

Plate 3714-A. Holder, china dish, vase
and cut glass tumbler . . . 9 00

Particular attention is directed to the new and very desirable series of holders — Plates 3709-A
to 3714-A—which have a minimum of metal to keep clean, combining simplicity, strength and good design.

All brass work of furnishings on pages 90 to 97 is nickel-plated. Discount on furnishings, pages
90 to 97, ten per cent.

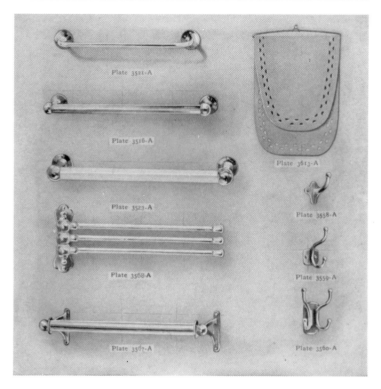

Plate 3568-A. Folding towel rack, three
bars, 12″ long $4 00
Same, three bars, 17″ long . . 4 40
Same, two bars, 12″ long . . . 3 25
Same, two bars, 17″ long . . 3 50

Plate 3567-A. Towel roller . . 3 20
Length over all, 20″; length of roller, 18¼″.

Plate 3523-A. Cellu-enamel 1″ Diam. 1½″ Diam.
(white) towel rod, 18″ long $2 75 $4 85
Same, 24″ long . . . 3 25 5 40
Same, 30″ long . . . 3 75 6 15

Plate 3516-A. Glass towel bar : Crystal Opaloid
1″ bar, 18″ long . . $2 25 $2 50
1″ bar, 24″ long . . 2 50 2 90
1″ bar, 30″ long . . 2 75 3 30
1½″ bar, 36″ long . . 7 50
1½″ bar, 42″ long . . 10 00
1½″ bar, 48″ long . . 10 75
1½″ bar, 54″ long . . 12 75
1½″ bar, 60″ long . . 13 75

Plate 3558-A. Robe hook . . . $0 25
Plate 3559-A. Robe hook . . . 0 50
Plate 3560-A. Robe hook . . . 1 00

Reg. Ex. Hvy.

Plate 3521-A. Brass towel rack :
No. 1. Length, 18″; width, 3″ $1 00 $1 25
No. 2. Length, 24″; width, 3″ 1 10 1 50
No. 3. Length, 30″; width, 3″ 1 75
No. 4. Length, 36″; width, 3″ 3 00
No. 5. Length, 48″; width, 3″ 4 75
No. 6. Length, 60″; width, 3″ 5 50

Plate 3613-A. Bath mats (rubber), for baths,
receptors and scales :
14″ x 11″ (scale mat) . . . $0 75
42″ x 15″ (5′ tub, regular width) . 3 35
48″ x 15″ (5½′ or 6′ tub, regular width) . 3 75
48″ x 18″ (6′, special width) . 4 85
27″ x 27″ (shower receptors, 36″) . 4 00
30″ x 30″ (shower receptors, 42″) . 4 35

Plate 3501-A. Shelf with guard rail and brackets:
Length, 24″; width, 5″ . . . $8 50
Length, 27″; width, 5″ . . . 8 75
Length, 30″; width, 5″ . . . 11 00

Plate 3517-A. Shelf with brackets :
No. 1. Length, 18″; width, 5″ . . 4 00
No. 2. Length, 24″; width, 5″ . . 4 50
No. 3. Length, 27″; width, 5″ . . 4 75
No. 4. Length, 30″; width, 5″ . . 5 00
No. 5. Length, 33″; width, 5″ . . 5 25
No. 6. Length, 36″; width, 5″ . . 5 50

Plate 3519-A. Plate glass shelf, with combination
brackets and holder, cut glass tumbler and china
vase :
No. 1. Length, 27″; width, 5″ . . $7 50
No. 2. Length, 30″; width, 5″ . . 7 75
No. 3. Length, 33″; width, 5″ . . 8 00

Plate 3508-A. China soap dish with holder 2 00

Plate 3509-A. Shelf, 27″ x 5″ x ½″
thick, with brackets and towel rack,
18″ long 7 25

Plate 3533-A. China soap dish with holder 3 05

Plate 3546-A. Holder for nail brush . 2 50

Plate 3707-A. China soap dish with holder 2 75

Plate 3708-A. Large china soap dish with
holder 3 50

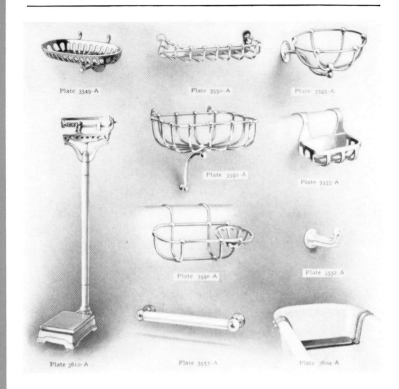

Plate 3549-A. Comb and brush holder . $5 50
Plate 3550-A. Comb and brush rack . 2 25
Plate 3552-A. China robe hook . . 0 20
Plate 3555-A. Soap dish for rim of bath
No. 1, 5″ x 3½″ 2 10
No. 2, 7½″ x 4½″ 3 15
When ordering state kind of bath for which soap dish is desired.
Plate 3557-A. Cellu-enamel hand rail, 24″ $4 50
Plate 3590-A. Sponge holder and soap dish for rim of bath 3 25
Plate 3592-A. Sponge holder . . 5 25

Plate 3595-A. Sponge holder . . . $2 40
Plate 3604-A. Adjustable oak bath seat . 8 00
Same, cellu-enamel 12 00
Plate 3610-A. Bathroom scale, white enameled 22 50
Same, with nickel-plated sliding measuring rod 31 00
Scale is furnished with cork platform mat.
Plate 3611-A. Bathroom scale, white enameled (see page 14) 36 75
Same, with n. p. standard and white enameled base 45 25

All brass work of furnishings on pages 90 to 97 is nickel-plated. Discount on furnishings, pages 90 to 97, ten per cent.

Plate 3634-A. Paper holder for sheets 8½″ x 5¾″ $3 00
Plate 3635-A. Recessed paper holder for 5¼″ x 3½″ roll 5 00
Plate 3636-A. Paper holder for roll paper 3 00
Plate 3643-A. Paper holder for 5¼″ x 3¼″ roll paper 2 65

Plate 3644-A. Paper holder for sheet paper, 8″ x 8″ $4 75
Plate 3650-A. Bathroom stool, white enamel finish 6 30
Same, cellu-enamel 10 00
Plate 3651-A. Cellu-enamel paper cabinet (sheets, 7¼″ x 5″) 12 00
Plate 3653-A. Bathroom Chair, cellu-enamel 25 00

All brass work of furnishings on pages 90 to 97 is nickel-plated. Discount on furnishings, pages 90 to 97, ten per cent.

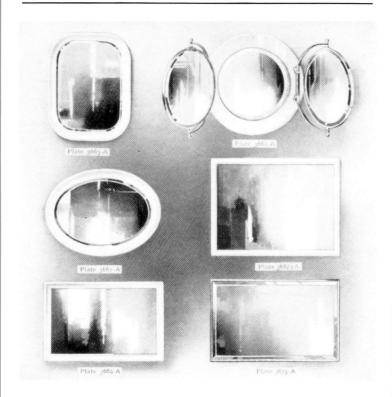

Plate 3663-A.

Plate 3662-A.

Plate 3661-A.

Plate 3682½-A.

Plate 3684-A.

Plate 3675-A.

Plate 3661-A. Beveled mirror with white enameled 2⅜″ wood frame, 30″ x 22″ . $20 00
Same, 33″ x 24″ 25 25
Same, 36″ x 27″ 29 50

Plate 3662-A. Round 12″ folding mirror with cellu-enamel frames . . . 24 00

Plate 3663-A. Beveled mirror with white enameled 2⅜″ wood frame, 30″ x 24″ . 23 50
Same, 36″ x 27″ 32 25
Same, 42″ x 30″ 38 00

Plate 3675-A. Beveled mirror with small brass frame, 24″ x 18″ . . . 15 00
Same, 27″ x 20″ 17 50
Same, 30″ x 22″ 19 00

Same, 33″ x 24″ $23 50
Same, 36″ x 27″ 28 25
Same, 60″ x 27″ 50 00
Same, 33″ x 24″, oval . . . 25 00
Same, 36″ x 27″, oval . . . 32 00

Plate 3684-A. Mirror (not beveled) with 1⅝″ white enameled wood frame, 24″ x 18″ 10 00
Same, 27″ x 20″ 11 25

Plate 3682½-A. Mirror (not beveled) with 1″ half-round white enameled wood frame, 24″ x 18″ 11 25
Same, 27″ x 20″ 13 00

When ordering, state whether mirrors are to be set vertical or horizontal.

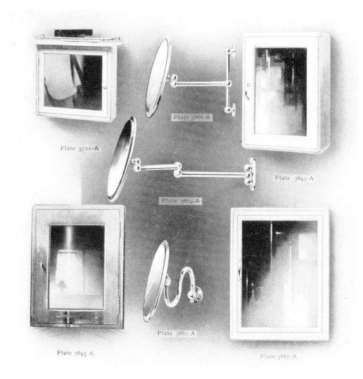

Plate 3701-A.

Plate 3668-A.

Plate 3693-A.

Plate 3669-A.

Plate 3667-A.

Plate 3695-A.

Plate 3687-A.

Plate 3667-A. Adjustable shaving mirror, 8″ x 10″ $8 75
Same, 10″ x 13″ 10 00
Same, round frame, 10″ x 10″ . . 10 75

Plate 3668-A. Adjustable 7″ shaving mirror 10 75

Plate 3669-A. Adjustable 7″ shaving mirror 10 75

Plate 3687-A. Recessed medicine cabinet with white enameled wood frame, porcelain-enameled iron receiver, mirror backed by brass plate, and adjustable glass shelves:
Size 1, 27¼″ x 21¼″ x 5″ . . 52 00
Size 2, 21¼″ x 15¾″ x 5″ . . 45 00

Plate 3693-A. White enameled medicine cabinet with plain mirror door and two adjustable plate glass shelves, 15½″ x 19½″ 12 10

Same, 18″ x 24″ $15 60
Same, 24″ x 30″ with three adjustable plate glass shelves 31 00
Same, cellu-enamel with beveled mirror door and two plate glass shelves (not adjustable), 18″ x 24″ . . 27 50
Same, 24″ x 30″ with three glass shelves 47 25

Plate 3695-A. Corner medicine cabinet, oak (varnish finish), with mirror (not beveled), 19″ x 24″ . . . 10 00
Same, polished finish . . . 11 50
Same, white enameled . . . 13 50
If with glass shelves instead of wood, add 3 50

Plate 3701-A. Toilet cabinet, white enameled, with mirror door, glass top and guard rail, 14″ x 17″ x 4½″ . . 19 50
Same, cellu-enamel 33 50
If with glass shelves instead of wood, add 1 60

Plate 1075-A, Modern Kitchen

THE above illustration shows some of the salient features of a well-appointed modern kitchen. Of course the size of a kitchen, also the various appointments, size and style of range, etc., depends largely on the size of the house. Sectional view shows ground plan of kitchen with butler's pantry and laundry.

For price of the "Barrington" kitchen sink, see page 100. Prices of the "Allston" vegetable sink, the "Muir" scullery sink, and utensil and towel racks, on application.

The "Defiance" combination coal and gas range, No. 87, with coal water-back, $160.00; if coal water-back is not required, deduct $6.50; add for French hood, $20.00.

Plate 1076-A

ENAMELED iron kitchen sinks can hardly be expected to be enduring when we consider the usage to which the average kitchen sink is subjected. There can be no question about the superiority in every respect of the imperial porcelain or colonial kitchen sinks, with their thickness of over two inches and their heavy glaze which covers not only the inside but the outside; still, to retain their fine appearance wood mats should always be used, so that pots and pans may not come in contact with the glazed surface, otherwise the sink will become more or less scratched or discolored, although its utility as a sink will not be affected.

For pantry sinks nothing is finer or more beautiful than imperial porcelain, although German silver or planished copper makes a durable and high-class fixture.

For some time we have practically given up the manufacture of the enameled iron wash tray, as it seemed to us that a porcelain vessel was the ideal and only one in which to wash fine linens and like fabrics, thus avoiding all danger of contact with rust through breakage or otherwise.

In view of various conflicting and specious claims made in recent years, we offer these comparisons and plain statements for the consideration of all who may be interested in plumbing fixtures.

Plate 7051-A

Plate 7051-A. The "Barrington" imperial porcelain kitchen sink, integral back and drain board, imperial porcelain legs, "Belknap" No. 4 n. p. ¾" compression faucet (china name-plates), 2" n. p. waste strainer and coupling, and wood mats for sink and drain board . . . .

	Imp. Porc.	
	Class A	Class B
	$124 55	$102 80

2" n. p. trap with waste to floor and vent to wall, extra, $10.25. For price of grease traps, see page 101. ¾" n. p. supply pipes with offsets and unions, extra, $8.50.

Length and width outside, 5' 1" x 2' 2"; sink inside, 32" x 20" x 6½" deep ; drain board, 2'; height of back, 9". "Belknap" faucet, 10½" centers.

Our imperial porcelain sinks are in appearance and from a sanitary and practical standpoint superior to all others. They are glazed white inside and outside. Strength and durability are assured by the substantial thickness of 2". They are made in one piece, without the joints so objectionable in a soapstone or slate sink. In the manufacture of large pieces of porcelain ware, some when taken out of the kiln are found to have slight marks or lines which do not detract from their general appearance or durability. These are termed Class B, and are recommended where cost is a consideration.

The "Barrington" sink is a most complete and desirable fixture. The back has space behind for the supply pipes ; it is ground so as to fit against the wall. Made only with drain board at left as shown.

Plate 7086-A. The "Ashland" imperial porcelain vegetable wash sink with integral back, imperial porcelain legs, "Belknap" No. 3 n. p. ⅝" compression faucet and n. p. "Simplex" standing waste and overflow . . . .

	Imp. Porc.	
	Class A	Class B
	$69 25	$53 75

1½" n. p. half S trap to wall, extra, $4.20. Ash cutting and drain board, 18" long, with n. p. hinges (shown on page 98), extra, $13.75.

Length and width outside, 30" x 22"; sink inside, 26" x 16½" x 9"; height of back, 9".

The vegetable wash sink, for thoroughly cleansing and preparing vegetables, is a necessary adjunct to the modern well-equipped kitchen.

Plate 7086-A

100

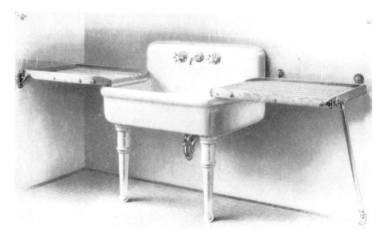

Plate 7054-A

Plate 7054-A. The "Rocona" kitchen sink, with integral back, legs, "Belknap" No. 4 n. p. ¾" compression faucet (china name-plates), 2" n. p. waste strainer and coupling, and wood mat, 24" x 22" x 7"

	Imp. Porc.		
	Class A	Class B	Colonial
24" x 22" x 7"	$44 05	$40 05	$33 05
Same, 27" x 22" x 7"	46 95	42 45	35 70
Same, 30" x 26" x 7"	60 15	47 40	39 00
Same, 36" x 26" x 7"	64 00	51 25	42 50
Same, 42" x 26" x 7"	75 35	58 60	51 35

Brass bent thimbles for faucet, extra, $1.10. 2" n. p. half S trap to wall, extra, $6.50. Ash drain board for corner, 30" long, with n. p. end hinges, as shown, extra, $14.50. Ash drain board for end, 30" long, with n. p. back hinges and telescopic leg, as shown, extra, $20.25. If with bronzed or painted iron legs, instead of imperial porcelain, deduct $3.00 ; instead of colonial, deduct $1.50.

Dimensions of sinks are outside, except depth, which is inside ; back, 9" high.

Plate 7344-A. "Tucker" grease trap. Size 1.
Height, 17"; diameter, 12¾"; painted cast iron $26 00
Same, enameled inside 33 00
Size 2. Height, 18¼"; diameter, 17¾"; painted cast iron 36 25
Same, enameled inside 47 25
Size 3. Height, 22"; diameter, 23⅜"; painted cast iron 55 00
Same, enameled inside 62 75
Size 4. Height, 17½"; diameter, 11½", nickel-plated 83 75
Size 1 and Size 4 are adapted for residences : Size 2 for large private residences, etc.; Size 3 for hotels, restaurants, etc.
Dimensions given above are outside.

Plate 7344-A
"Tucker" Grease Trap

The "Tucker" grease trap is composed of an inner chamber into which the waste water and grease passes, and an outer chamber through which the cold water supply for the house flows. The circulation of cold water around the outside, chills or congeals the grease entering into the inner chamber; the grease being lighter than water, gathers at the top and is thus prevented from passing through the outlet. The central partition is an important feature in that it increases the area of cooling surface and also deflects the waste water upward, consequently bringing it in contact with a greater amount of cooling surface before it passes through the outlet.

The "Tucker" trap is unquestionably the best grease trap made.

101

76

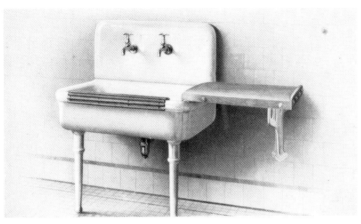

Plate 7064-A

Imp. Porc.

Plate 7064-A. The "Chelsea" kitchen sink with legs, back 18″ high, n. p. "Harlem" ⅝″ compression faucets (with china name-plates, cold faucet with hose end) and 2″ waste strainer with coupling,

	Class A	Class B	Colonial
30″ x 20″ x 7″	$37 45	$32 95	$25 20
Same, 30″ x 24″ x 7″	42 45	33 70	26 70
Same, 36″ x 23″ x 7″	46 20	36 95	27 70

Wood mat with rim guard, as shown, extra, for 30″ sink, $4.25 ; 36″, $5.25 ; 2″ n. p. half S trap to wall, extra, $6.50. Ash drain board, 30″ long, with bronzed iron bracket, as shown, extra, $9.00. If with bronzed or painted iron legs, instead of imperial porcelain, deduct, $3.00 ; instead of colonial, deduct $1.50. For price of grease traps, see page 101.

Plate 7300-A. The "Beekman" roll-rim iron kitchen sink with integral back and concealed "Simplex" hanger,

	Galv.	Enam.
24″ x 18″ x 6″	$10 25	$11 25
Same, 27″ x 18″ x 6″	11 00	12 25
Same, 30″ x 18″ x 6″	12 00	13 25
Same, 30″ x 20″ x 6″	12 50	14 25
Same, 36″ x 21″ x 6″	15 00	16 50

Height of back, 12″.

If with legs instead of "Simplex" hanger, add, for galvanized sink, $2.40; enameled sink, $2.00.

State whether right or left drain board is required.

Note—With enameled iron sinks bronzed iron legs are furnished.

If with enameled iron legs, add $1.70.

Enameled iron, 18″x25″ drain board with bronzed iron bracket, $5.65. "Harlem" n. p. ⅝″ compression sink faucets with china name-plates (cold faucet with hose end), per pair, $3.00. 2″ galvanized iron half S trap, $2.25. 2″ n.p. brass half S trap with inlet to connect sink collar to trap, $6.25. Air chambers, each, extra, plain $1.15 ; galvanized, $1.35.

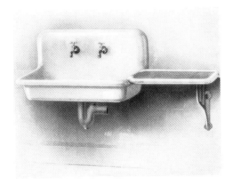

Plate 7300-A

Plate 7336-A

Plate 7336-A. The "Belgrade" enameled iron kitchen sink combination with integral apron, drain board and back, concealed wall hanger, adjustable enameled iron legs, n. p. waste strainer and coupling, n. p. "Harlem" ⅝″ compression faucets with china name-plates, and n. p. 1½″ half S trap with i. p. size waste to wall and two wood mats for sink and drain board, as Plate 7094-A $47 00

If with tubing waste to wall, deduct 0 35

If with "Belknap" No. 4 n. p. combination supply faucet with china name-plates, as Plate 7704-A, add 7 50

If less faucets and trap, deduct 7 45

Dimensions—Length over all, 4′ 5″; width, 20¼″; height of back, 12″; sink, 26″ x 16″ x 5″, inside; drain board, 24″; apron, 5½″.

Note—The "Belgrade" may be furnished with right or left drain board; when ordering state if sink is desired with left drain board, as shown, or with right drain board.

Plate 7704-A

Plate 7094-A

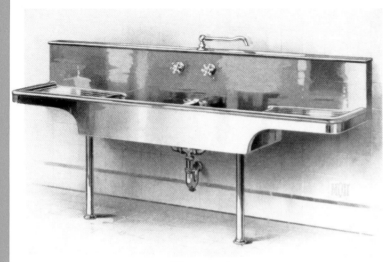

Plate 7100-A

Plate 7100-A. The "Pelham" white metal double pantry sink with drain board, dividing partition, back and apron, white metal compression supply valve (china name-plates) with movable nozzle with shut-off, white metal legs, standing wastes and overflows, and twin waste connection with 2" half S trap to wall $460 25
Same, heavy copper, with red metal fittings 389 00
Dimensions—Length over all, 6' 5½"; width, front to back, 27"; height of back, 12"; depth inside, 7"; width of roll-rim, 2".
Every detail of the "Pelham" pantry sink is first class. The copper or white metal is heavy, and covers not only the top and front of the sink, but also the bottom. Joints or seams are eliminated wherever possible, but, where necessary, are so skillfully made as to be almost invisible.
Prices of "Pelham" and "Plymouth" pantry sinks in other sizes, also with right or left ends for corners, or both ends for recesses, are furnished on application.

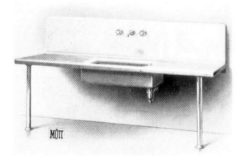

Plate 7102-A

Plate 7102-A. The "Plymouth" pantry sink, comprising ash top and drain board, n. p. legs, Italian marble back, tinned copper sink with oak casing and n. p. "Simplex" standing waste and overflow, "Belknap" No. 4 n. p. ⅝" faucet, and n.p. 1½" half S trap to wall 84 75
Same, German silver with n. p. fittings . . . 105 25
Same, white metal with n. p. fittings . . . 133 00
Dimensions—Length of ash top, 6'; width, 27"; sink proper, 24" x 18"; height of back, 16".

Plate 7068-A

Imp. Porc.
Class A Class B

Plate 7068-A. The "Brunswick" imperial porcelain pantry sink with integral back and drain board, imperial porcelain legs, "Belknap" No. 4 n. p. ¾" compression faucet (china name-plates), n. p. "Simplex" standing waste and overflow and wood mats for sink and drain board $129 75 $104 50

1½" n. p. trap with waste to floor and vent to wall, extra, $6.75

For prices of grease traps, see page 101.

The "Brunswick" sink is made only with drain board at left as shown.

Dimensions—Length and width outside, 5' 1" x 2' 2"; sink inside, 25" x 20" x 6½" deep; height of back, 9"; length of drain board, 31".

Plate 7070-A. The "Pierrepont" imperial porcelain pantry sink with integral back, imperial porcelain legs, "Belknap" No. 4 n. p. ¾" compression faucet (china name-plates), n. p. "Simplex" standing waste and overflow and wood mat, 27" x 22" x 7" 50 55 46 30
Same, 30" x 26" x 7" 68 25 52 75

1½" n. p. half S trap to wall, extra . . . $4 20

For price of grease traps, see page 101.

Ash drain board for corner, 30" long, recessed for waste, with n. p. end hinges as shown, extra . 16 75

Ash drain board, 30" long, with n. p. back hinges and telescopic leg, as shown, extra . . . 20 25

Note—The "Pierrepont" sink can only be furnished with recess at left end as shown.

Dimensions of sinks are outside, except depth, which is inside; back, 9" high.

Plate 7070-A

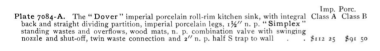

Imp. Porc.
Class A   Class B

Plate 7084-A. The "**Dover**" imperial porcelain roll-rim kitchen sink, with integral back and straight dividing partition, imperial porcelain legs, 1½" n. p. "**Simplex**" standing wastes and overflows, wood mats, n. p. combination valve with swinging nozzle and shut-off, twin waste connection and 2" n. p. half S trap to wall . . $112 25 $91 50

Ash drain board for corner, 30" long, with n. p. end hinges, extra 14 50

Ash drain board for end, 30" long, with n. p. back hinges and telescopic leg, extra . 20 25

Dimensions—Length outside, 42"; width outside, 26"; sinks inside, 20" x 17½" x 7"; height of back, 9".

The swinging nozzle with shut-off for double sinks is an important feature; when water is turned on at the valves and the goose neck is directly in line with the partition the water supply is shut off, but as the nozzle is swung either to the right or left the water is turned on.

Our imperial porcelain sinks are in appearance and from a sanitary and practical standpoint superior to all others. They are glazed white inside and outside. Strength and durability are assured by the substantial thickness of 2". They are made in one piece, without the joints so objectionable in a soapstone or slate sink. In the manufacture of large pieces of porcelain ware, some when taken out of the kiln are found to have slight marks or lines which do not detract from their general appearance or durability. These are termed Class B, and are recommended where cost is a consideration.

Imp. Porc.
Class A   Class B

Plate 7615-A. The "**Wadsworth**" imperial porcelain roll-rim kitchen sink and wash tub combination with integral back and imperial porcelain legs, n. p. sink strainer, n. p. wash tub plug and stopper, ⅝" n. p. "**Harlem**" compression sink faucets with china name-plates, ½" n. p. "**Harlem**" compression wash tub faucets with tee handles and combination ash swinging cover and drain board . . $100 25 $77 25

2" n. p. waste pipe and 2" trap, with i. p. size waste to wall, extra $18 75

1½" n. p. waste pipe and 2" trap, with i. p. size waste to wall, extra 12 25

Ash drain board, 30" long, with n. p. back hinges and telescopic leg, as shown, extra . 20 25

Dimensions—Length, 4'; width, 1' 11"; height of back, 6"; depth of sink, 7"; depth of tub, 14".

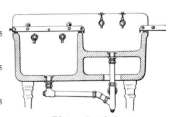

Plate 7615½-A

Longitudinal section of "**Wadsworth**" sink and wash tub combination

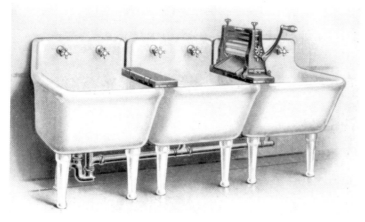

Plate 7602-A

Plate 7612-A

Plate 7602-A. The "**Wentworth**" roll-rim wash tubs with integral backs (ground), legs and wringer base (patented), per set of two, Size 1

	Imp. Porc. Class A	Class B	Colonial
Plate 7602-A. The "Wentworth" roll-rim wash tubs with integral backs (ground), legs and wringer base (patented), per set of two, Size 1	$71 10	$62 60	$48 10
Same, per set of two, Size 2	92 80	71 10	55 60
Same, per set of three, Size 1	109 65	96 90	75 15
Same, per set of three, Size 2	142 20	109 65	86 40

If with painted or bronzed iron legs, deduct for each tub, imperial porcelain, $3.00; colonial, $1.50; ⅝" n. p. compression faucets, as shown, per pair, $4.50; cast-brass n. p. waste plug with n. p. stopper, each, $1.40. Mott's special wringer, $7.75.

Dimensions—Length of each tub from right to left, Size 1, 2'; Size 2, 2' 7½"; width from front to back, 2' 3"; depth inside, 1' 3"; height of back, 6". The integral backs are recessed behind with room for the pipes and are ground to fit against the wall.

Plate 7530-A. The "**Hanover**" roll-rim slop sink with integral back, n. p. strainer, bronzed iron trap-standard and ⅝" n. p. "**Harlem**" compression faucets with china name-plates, 20" x 18" x 12"

	Imp. Porc. Class A	Class B	Colonial
...20" x 18" x 12"	$36 75	$32 50	$27 25
Same, 22" x 20" x 12"	41 00	36 00	31 25
Same, 24" x 22" x 12"	45 50	39 50	34 25
If with vitreous porcelain trap-standard, No. 10 brass floor flange and porcelain bolt caps, add			9 25
Brass bent thimbles for faucets, extra, per pair			1 10
If with "Belknap" n. p. No. 4 ⅝" faucet, as Plate 7070-A (page 105), add			6 00

Spring rim guard, n. p., extra, 20", $13.00; 22", $13.50; 24", $14.00.

Dimensions—Above dimensions are outside, except depth, which is inside; height of back, 12".

When ordering, state if trap is to be with or without hub vent; also, if for lead or iron waste pipe.

Plate 7530-A

Plate 7612-A. The "**Warren**" wash tubs with bronzed iron standards and ash top, per set of two, Size 1

	Imp. Porc. Class A	Class B	Colonial
Plate 7612-A. The "Warren" wash tubs with bronzed iron standards and ash top, per set of two, Size 1	$31 50	$26 70	$20 60
Same, per set of two, Size 2	46 20	29 50	23 20
Same, per set of three, Size 1	46 55	39 35	30 20
Same, per set of three, Size 2	68 60	43 55	34 10

½" n. p. "**Harlem**" compression wash tub faucets with tee handle, per pair, $1.50. Cast-brass n. p. waste plug with n. p. stopper, each, $1.40. 1½" n. p. waste pipe with 2" trap for two tubs, $14.00; for three tubs, $18.25. Mott's special wringer, $7.75. Portable ash covers, each, extra, size 1, $2.15; size 2, $2.35.

Stamped brass n. p. plug with n. p. stopper, each $0.60.

Length, Size 1, 24"; Size 2, 30"; width from front to back, 26"; depth inside, 15".

Porcelain ware, with its substantial thickness, fine glaze and beautiful appearance, is pre-eminently the ideal material for sanitary appliances, such as wash tubs, etc. The prices are such that the tubs can be used in all fine and moderate-priced dwellings.

The colonial wash tubs are excellent where cost is a consideration. They are light buff in color, glazed inside and outside, easily kept clean, practically everlasting, low in price and infinitely superior to enameled cast iron.

Plate 7525-A. The "**Ralston**" roll-rim iron slop sink with integral back, combination trap-standard, n. p. strainer and n. p. ⅝" "**Harlem**" compression faucets with china name-plates (cold faucet with hose end), 22" x 18" x 12"

	Painted	Galv.	Enam.
...22" x 18" x 12"	$15 50	$20 50	$26 00
Same, 24" x 20" x 12"	18 00	23 00	28 50
If without faucets, deduct	3 00		
If with brass floor flange for lead connection, add	1 75		

When ordering, state if trap is to be with or without hub vent; also, if outlet is for lead or iron waste pipe.

Plate 7525-A

INDEX

EIGHTY-SIX YEARS
OF SUPREMACY
1828-1914

THE name of "Mott" has been for nearly a century a synonym for the highest grade plumbing goods at a moderate price. This mere statement carries with it full assurance as to the quality, durability and uniform excellence of our products. At all expositions where our goods have been exhibited, we have received the highest awards.

AMERICAN STANDARD

American Standard is the result of successive mergers by a number of companies. The oldest was Arens and Ott Manufacturing of Louisville, which began producing cast-iron soil pipes in 1857. A second important firm was the Standard Manufacturing Company of Allegheny, Pa., founded in 1870 as a manufacturer of enameled cast-iron stove ware. A third firm was begun in 1887 by Edward L. Dawes, a Standard employee who left to begin an enameling manufactory with William A. Myler in New Brighton, Pa. By 1893 Dawes and Myler were producing enameled cast-iron bathtubs exclusively. In 1899 these three major firms — Arens and Ott, Standard Manufacturing Company and Dawes and Myler — merged with six smaller companies to form the Standard Sanitary Manufacturing Company, which became a major producer of enameled cast-iron bathroom fixtures. Ceramic fixtures were not part of Standard's production, but were added in 1929, when the firm acquired Thomas Maddock's Sons Company. This firm had its origins in 1873, when Thomas Maddock, a pottery painter from Staffordshire, England, became a partner in a Trenton, N.J., pottery that was the first in America to produce heavy sanitary ware such as toilet and sink bowls. In one other significant business venture, the Standard Sanitary Manufacturing Company in 1929 formed a partnership with the American Radiator Company of New York City under the name American Radiator and Standard Sanitary Corporation, today known as American Standard.

"Standard"

Planning your Plumbing wisely

"Standard"
PLUMBING FIXTURES
for the HOME

A beautiful bathroom is so easy to plan if you visit a "Standard" Plumbing Fixture display.

Plan Wisely! Choose Well!
Enjoy the Conveniences of a Lovely Bathroom!

YOU want your home to be comfortable and attractive. You want the conveniences that present-day science, engineering and designing skill have created for all phases of modern living. Then, by all means start in the bathroom, the health center of the home.

Today's mode of living is made possible only with adequate and capably installed plumbing. And all the benefits of modern plumbing are not *fully* realized unless the fixtures and the room arrangement are in keeping with the recent rapid advances in design and decoration.

If your home is still on the Architect's or Builder's blue prints—then enjoy to the full the thrill of planning from the start a bathroom that will give rein to your most cherished ideas. Never before have experts in all phases of bathroom planning laid before you such an array of ideas and materials. New plumbing fixture forms, color, the sparkle of glass and metal, the utility and the beauty of new floor and wall materials, a host of modern ideas for room arrangement and decoration . . . all these are yours today, at costs that do not exceed the outlays for the commonplaces of yesterday.

If your bathroom is old and out dated, then you will be pleased to know that you, too, can plan to use these modern improvements. They can easily be installed in a present bathroom, in one planned from an old hall end or part of another room, or in a double service bathroom (page 4).

The essential thing is to plan wisely—consider all phases of your bathroom problem, use the services of your Master Plumber, your Builder and the representatives of the manufacturers of the fixtures and other materials. Remember, that in bathroom planning the important thing is that the room be built around the fixtures. They are the principal reason for the room's existence, all its decoration must be inspired by and be centered about them.

Choose well! Consider plumbing fixture quality, design, reputation, good installation, long service, lasting beauty. And none offer higher quality, wider variety of beautiful designs and color, finer reputation—and at as reasonable cost as any—than do "Standard" Plumbing Fixtures, with the record of nearly a half a century of manufacture and satisfactory performance to recommend them.

I

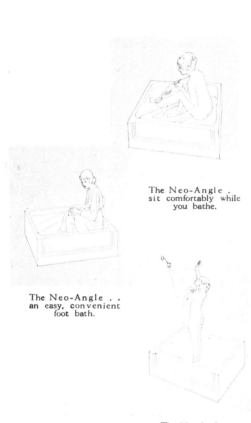

The Neo-Angle .
sit comfortably while
you bathe.

The Neo-Angle . .
an easy, convenient
foot bath.

The Neo-Angle . .
ample elbow room.

Fixtures: Neo-Angle Bath, P 2105 E R, (lever handles)
Companion Lavatory
Master One-Piece Closet

2

THE NEO-ANGLE BATH

Can you conceive of a decorative plan for any other room of the home that will not be matched favorably by the attractive Penthouse Bathroom Group on the opposite page? The room as shown is in keeping with the sumptuousness of the finest of homes or apartments, but this bathroom can be comfortably large in a space ten feet square.

The floor in the illustration is rubber, the walls shaded linoleum, the fixture color is Corallin, and the bath is the sensational, entirely new Neo-Angle, which in a few months revolutionized bathroom planning.

If distinction and convenience are both essential, you must decide on the Neo-Angle. No other bath is such an all-purpose, all-age, all-condition bath. It is only 4 feet square, yet it has more bathing space than the present known 5 foot long types.

The two seats in the corners are responsible for many new features—you can enter and leave the bath safely in a sitting position, you can take a shower while sitting, you can remain seated while tub bathing or washing the feet. There is plenty of elbow room for either tub bath or shower. What a boon are all these features to elderly bathers, to invalids or tired bathers of any age.

While Neo-Angle discharges every practical function more perfectly than any other existing bath, it also opens up a whole realm of decorative possibilities. First, it lends itself to a more artistic grouping of necessary bathroom fixtures. Being available in the full range of "Standard" colors, it gives unbridled rein to your color preferences.

Moreover, a new decorative treatment becomes possible and a new saving in the lessened need for water-proof materials. Only the walls immediately adjacent to the bath need be of water-proof materials because the ample receptor feature, made possible by the greater width of the Neo-Angle Bath, largely confines water splashing to the tub recess. For the rest of the room delicate fabrics and textured floor coverings may be introduced with safety.

Notice the unusualness of the installation opposite. The plate glass can be replaced by a built-up wall if desired, or if a recess is not preferred, the corner pattern of the Neo-Angle, illustrated on page 18, can be used.

The Neo-Angle...leave or enter safely and with ease.

The Neo-Angle . . . a carefree shower no slipping.

The Neo-Angle . . . plenty of space for immersion.

3

The Two-in-One Group

Had you ever imagined that a bathroom of such distinction with the practical uses of two bathrooms, could be built in a space as small as ten feet square. Well, here it is! The Neo-Angle Bath is in its own compartment with a door to each room. A beautiful Vitreous China lavatory and quiet, attractive Master One-Piece Closet are in each of the rooms outside the bath compartment. Note that three fixture colors are used, but the entire ensemble is in harmony. It is a novel and most efficient use of space.

Fixtures:
Neo-Angle Bath, P 2100 E
Blackford, Roxbury Lavatories
Master One-Piece Closets

4

PLANNING THE BATHROOM

Have you suppressed the need and the desire for a new bathroom to replace your present one, have you stinted the bathroom planned for your new home—all because you have believed that cost would be excessive? Don't let this worry you any longer.

With the limitless variety of long-used and of newly designed materials for walls and floors, and with the extensive variety of "Standard" Plumbing Fixtures, you can achieve a distinctive bathroom no matter what your budget.

Floors are now of tile or other vitrified material, rubber, linoleum, even carpet. Walls are plain finish with water-proofing only on areas within splashing range of fixtures. These can be of tile or glass, linoleum or water-proofed papers. Accessories such as cabinets, mirrors, lighting fixtures, towel bars, are procurable in a host of types and designs. With all of these you can exercise a wide freedom of choice and get something distinctive in any price range.

Color in plumbing fixtures is not costly—in fact it is but a small part of the total cost of any bathroom. Used correctly, it is by far the most economical means of attaining individuality in bathroom furnishing and decoration.

In originating the color composition, keep in mind the value of simplicity. The starting point should be the selection of the color for the plumbing fixtures. That should always be the key color. Then you can select colors for the walls, floor and draperies which will contrast harmoniously with the fixtures.

When you are ready to remodel your old bathroom or build a new one you will find that good taste in the selection and use of the plumbing fixtures and materials is more important than the price you pay for them. Don't delay—plan to go ahead with your bathroom *now.*

TIME PAYMENT PLAN

In keeping with the NATIONAL HOUSING ACT, the Standard Sanitary Mfg. Co. has a new finance plan with the lowest rates ever made available—one to three years to pay, no red tape, no mortgage, no co-makers or endorsers; only the signatures of the property owners are required. This plan complies with the government requirements and the transactions are handled through the Heating and Plumbing Finance Corporation, one of the first to be approved by the FHA.

To finance a loan of $120 to $2000 for modernizing your bathroom, kitchen or laundry with beautiful, serviceable "Standard" Plumbing Fixtures, get an estimate of complete cost, fill out an application and sign a note for the deferred balance. The installation is quickly made and you pay in monthly installments of $10 or more for one to three years. Your Master Plumber will gladly handle all details. Purchasers desiring to use the regular finance plan of the Heating and Plumbing Finance Corporation can still do so.

5

The Chateau Group

Chaste dignity is here achieved with straight lines in the architectural design of the room and the recessing of Bath and Lavatory. Where it is not practical to recess the lavatory, an unusual touch can be gained by selecting the Tubular Lavatory, F 112 G, as shown in circle. The Moderno Closet of paneled design and low set tank, eliminating from view the customary flush pipe connection, is attractive and very modern. This room is a good example of the excellent use of water-proofed materials where required, and customary materials elsewhere.

Tubular Vitreous China Lavatory 24 x 20 inches Chromard frame 20 inches long.

Fixtures: Pembroke Recess Bath
Clyde Lavatory
Moderno Closet

6

Make Your Bathroom Livable

It is so easy to have more than just a bathroom—so much more satisfying, with a little extra planning and expenditure —to develop a room of cheer, of beauty, and extra utility.

Many owners are adding more space than was formerly allotted to the bath, and now install in addition to the fixtures, sun-lamps, health apparatus, dressing tables, etc. And rightly so! The bathroom is the intimate room—why shouldn't provisions be made for these distinctly personal touches of modern life?

Use simple decorations, use materials that will stand moisture and vapor and that are easily cleaned—use some color, in the decoration, the draperies, and in the fixtures—use "Standard" Plumbing Fixtures, for assured beauty and long life.

"Standard" fixtures are available in a variety of colors, to meet every decorative need. The cost, considering the results obtained, is very little more than for white. Your Master Plumber can give or arrange for helpful suggestions in color use and in the problems of room decoration.

An extra bathroom adds so much more convenience to your home, makes its routine smoother and more pleasant. It avoids irritating delays and inconvenience during the morning and evening busy periods of bathroom use.

Guests, too, remember their visits and appreciate the true hospitality which another bathroom for their own use affords. It need not be an elaborate one, for again the wide variety of "Standard" designs and the many usable wall and floor materials, allow easy planning of a second, livable bathroom.

The Villa Group

This is the ideal ensemble for the small bathroom. These are all comparatively inexpensive fixtures. The room is simple, water-proofed materials are used only where needed, and color has added a charm far beyond its little extra cost. Even with the fixtures in white, the colorful walls and floor assure a distinctive bathroom.

Fixtures: Pembroke Bath, Hexagon Lavatory, Siacto Closet

The Apartment Group

This group presents an idea that is growing in favor —that of placing the water-closet in a separate compartment. Rubber floor, a striking water-proofed wall covering and "Standard" fixtures in color combine to create an attractive room.
The recessed glass panel in back of the bath reflecting, mirror like, the rest of the room, creates a feeling of spaciousness.

Fixtures: Pembroke Bath, Hibben Lavatory, Compact Closet

7

The Neo-Mode Group

Does your bathroom look like the one below? Possibly not, but you surely have seen a similar room in many homes that now have up-to-date heating, refrigeration, etc.

There is certainly no need for such a room any longer, when modern **"Standard"** fixtures, linoleum or tile floor, linoleum or wall paper walls can transform it, at a very reasonable cost, into the beautiful distinctive room at the right. When a recess for the bath is not available, the Neo-Angle Bath, corner pattern, permits the same up-to the minute modernization of your bathroom.

Before:
Old fashioned —unsightly— an irritation to the family.

After: Beautiful—modern—clean—inviting —easy to keep spick and span.

Fixtures: Neo-Angle Bath P 2100 E
Neolyn Lavatory
One-Piece Closet

8

REMODEL INEXPENSIVELY

There is no room in the house which can be changed from drabness to beauty, from cheerlessness to enviable charm, from prosaic utility to inviting usefulness, with such ease, such satisfaction and at such reasonable cost . . . as the bathroom.

Of course, the bathroom in a new home is a major investment but new fixtures in an old bathroom give the same thrill —and how easily and inexpensively it is accomplished.

A remodeled bathroom gives more than increased beauty and convenience—it actually adds its cost to the value of the house. It hastens the sale, should you ever decide to sell, because every new owner now insists upon a modern, beautiful and convenient bathroom. In fact every far-seeing purchaser demands at least two bathrooms.

Unless the supply and drainage pipes in walls and floor have deteriorated the installation of new fixtures is a simple matter. Just imagine the old fixtures replaced with glossy white or sparkling colored fixtures of distinctive, modern design. Renew the old drab bathroom that no amount of effort seems to improve. Especially replace the old noisy toilet with either the attractive, quiet "Standard" One-Piece or Compact Closet.

With such a variety of attractive, yet inexpensive fixtures and decorative materials, you can also plan to have that second bathroom, that extra toilet room to which growing families and guests are entitled. Your Master Plumber can show you how easily you can remodel your present bathroom, how little space is required to install a second one.

Improved materials and more efficient methods for plumbing installation make it easier now than ever before to go ahead with your postponed plans.

Time Payments, described on page 5, remove the last objection to immediate remodeling.

Notice in the "Before" and "After" illustrations here,

Simple architectural changes in this room and modern fixtures have altered an ordinary prosaic arrangement into this "transformation" bathroom of unusual character and beauty.

how a colorful tile floor and wall and a re-arrangement of new, inexpensive fixtures have transformed this simple bathroom. Bright, non-tarnishing Chromard finish for the graceful brass fittings adds a sparkling note that is sure to satisfy. The new fixtures are: Pembroke Bath, Buena Lavatory F 337 G, and Compact Closet.

9

The
Manor Group

See in this bathroom how "Standard" designers have given you complete harmony of fixture line. Only when all the fixtures are made by one producer can you expect to secure this harmony, so essential to good room planning.

The Manor Group is becoming increasingly popular. It is modern, convenient, compact — and you can have the beauty and utility of these three attractive fixtures in a space no larger than 6 by 8 feet.

The lavatory is the Companion, F 115 FQ. It is available in the 22″ and 26″ sizes, and has towel bars between the front legs and supporting brackets. These bars are a new and welcome convenience, as they provide the proper location for towels, handy when needed, yet out of the way when not in use.

Chesterton Lavatory
Five Sizes, see pages 12, 13

Fixtures: Pembroke Bath
One-Piece Closet
Companion Lavatory

10

Vitreous China Lavatories

Of all the fixtures in the bathroom, the lavatory offers the widest latitude for expressing the owner's ideas of design. Have you in mind a practically square or an extremely wide lavatory, or one with round corners, or with cut-off corners? Then you can have it. Do you prefer a pedestal base or center china leg or slender Chromard legs? Then you will find your preference, with the type of top section you like in combination with a number of leg and pedestal supports, to suit your every requirement.

There is a *"Standard"* Vitreous China Lavatory for every type of bathroom, large or small. The unusually large Chesterton, with flat top 42 inches wide, illustrated separately on page 10; the deluxe Templeton (page 32) and the kindred Pemberton design, the Castleton, the Tubular, the Strate-line—all are distinctive china lavatories for the luxurious bathroom. For the bathroom of more usual size, a variety of designs range from 30 x 24" to 14 x 14" in size.

And whatever *"Standard"* china lavatory you select, remember that it will be extremely hard, smooth and non-absorbent. It will afford the utmost ease in cleaning and will not be marred or discolored by medicines or liquid cleansers. Cleaning powders should be selected with care as gritty cleansers will affect any glossy surface.

"Standard" lavatories in color are exquisitely beautiful. Here, again, is found the necessity of using fixtures from one producer, as the color of the lavatory, of vitreous china and that of the bath, of enameled iron, can be expected to match only if they come from the same manufacturer.

The Companion Lavatory - F 115 F
SIZES: 26 x 22", 22½ x 18"

11

Towerlyn - F 110 G

Chesterton - F 80 G

Marlton - F 315 F

Here for ready comparison is spread out leading examples of the many **"Standard"** Vitreous China Lavatories. The Chesterton and Castleton have cast brass Chromard Finish legs; the Castleton has a unit supply fitting. The Roxbury and Strateline are more economically priced leg designs. The Towerlyn is a very distinctive pedestal lavatory, in complete harmony of line with the Pembroke and Neo-Angle bath; the Brainard and Blackford are more commonly used pedestal types. The Randall and Hibben are supported by a center leg. The other lavatories shown are supported entirely from the wall.

The Companion, here shown, is the same lavatory as that illustrated in a number of bathrooms except without legs. With legs it has the fixture number F 115 F, (page 11) and with legs and side towel rails, F 115 F Q (page 10). The Marlton and Marcosa are two space saving designs.

Blackford - F 117 G

Roxbury - F 131 G

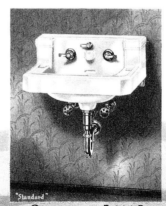

Companion - F 116 F

Lucerne - F 367 WZ

12

The Denlava is a new but essential bathroom dental fixture for all who give more than ordinary thought to hygenic conditions.

Notice that these lavatories are shown with all-metal fittings. The development of non-tarnishing Chromard has made popular this type of fitting, but fittings with china handles and escutcheons in white or color, can be had if preferred.

Your Master Plumber can give you installed prices for any *"Standard"* lavatory. He can help you in selecting proper fixtures, choosing colors and designs that harmonize. Consult him *first*.

SIZES: — *Towerlyn; 24 x 20", 27 x 22", 30 x 24". Chesterton; 24 x 20", 27 x 22", 30 x 24", 36 x 22", 42 x 22". Blackford and Roxbury; 24 x 20", 27 x 22", 30 x 24". Companion; F 116 F, 22 x 18"; F 115 F and F 115 F Q, 22 x 18", 26 x 22". Castleton; 30 x 22". Brainard; 24 x 20", 27 x 22", 30 x 24". Lucerne; 20 x 18", 24 x 20". Strate-line; 24 x 20". Marcosa; 26 x 14", 20 x 13". Marlton; 26 x 15". Denlava; 16 x 16". Randall; 20 x 18", 24 x 20". Hibben; 20 x 18", 24 x 20", 27 x 22".*

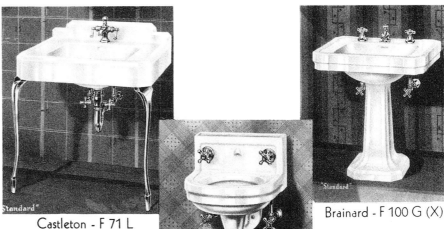

Castleton - F 71 L

Denlava - F 575 G

Brainard - F 100 G (X)

Strate-line - F 114 G

Marcosa - F 319 RZ

Hibben - F 217 B

Randall - F 270 W

13

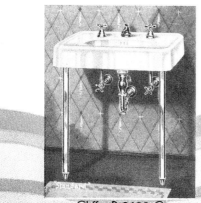

Clyde - P 3127 G

As all **"Standard"** Plumbing Fixtures are of one uniform quality, the best that experience and large resources can produce, there is no question here as to kind of material. Just as certain designs lend themselves best to reproduction in vitreous china so also **"Standard"** Enameled Lavatories are the finest examples of designs best produced in enameled cast-iron. They are available in either regular enamel, or in Acid-Resisting Enamel which is comparable to vitreous china in its resistance to stain or discoloration by acids, medicines, etc. Both types of enameled fixtures are slightly cheaper than vitreous china. Where a careful budget is a factor, regular enamel with reasonable care will give good service. It should

always be borne in mind that any plumbing fixture of whatever material can be marred by harsh, gritty cleansers which should never be used.

An extensive variety of enameled lavatories, (the most widely used shown here) is available, particularly for the smaller bathrooms. The Cliff, Clyde and Hexagon are leg, pedestal and wall hanging lavatories which follow the present trend to cut-off corner design. The Laton harmonizes with the lines of the Pembroke Bath, the Marco is a space saving design, the Anglo is for installation in a corner. The Othello, P 4209 M, illustrates a unit fitting, supplying hot, cold or tempered water from the one spout. This fitting

Cliff - P 3122 G

Hexagon - P 3867 BZ

Marco - P 4219 SZ

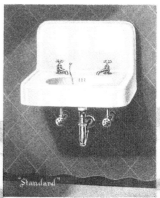

Ophir - P 3845 R

14

"Standard" Enameled Lavatories

can be had for a number of enameled and vitreous china lavatories.

Notice the variety of fitting arrangements offered in the vitreous china and enameled cast-iron lavatory groups. Tempered water types, with hot, cold or mixed water flowing through a single spout provide the most satisfactory form of supply, and permit one to wash in running water. Lavatories shown with single faucets can generally be had with either a pop-up drain operated by a lift knob or with chain and rubber stopper.

These lavatories are shown with **"Standard"** cast brass traps. The trap is important as it is your safeguard from sewer gas. A cast brass trap with cleanout is strong and sturdy, will last for years

and more than pays for its little extra cost in beauty and service.

Your Master Plumber can give you installed prices for any **"Standard"** lavatory. Through study, training and practical experience, Master Plumbers are the only ones qualified to install or supervise the proper installation of Plumbing Fixtures. It has been truly said, "The Plumber Protects the Health of the Nation."

SIZES:

Cliff, Clyde, and Laton, 24 x 20", 27 x 22"; *Hexagon*, 20 x 18", 22 x 19"; *Ophir*, 21 x 17", 24 x 18"; *Othello*, P 4205 R, 19 x 17", 21 x 18"; *Othello*, P 4209 M, 21 x 18"; *Marco*, 26 x 14"; *Anglo*, 16 x 16", 19 x 19"; *Beverly*, 19 x 17", 21 x 18".

Laton   P 3117 G

Othello - P 4205 R

Othello - P 4209 M

Beverly - P 4335 R

Anglo - P 4955 R

15

"Standard" Baths
Provide That Touch of Distinction

If you have a flair for distinction in design, the distinction that comes from modern treatment on correct lines, you will like the Neo-Classic motif that is the basis of Neo-Angle, Neo-Classic Pembroke and other **"Standard"** Baths. But of all baths, none can compare with the Neo-Angle here depicted. Distinguished . . . uncommon . . . a sense of true luxury is attained in this first real improvement in bath design in many years. There is a **"Standard"** Bath for every purpose, and for every size bathroom. There is even a built-in bath as small as 43 inches long by 29 inches wide. Built-in types are available for tiling into one wall, two walls, three walls or as free standing baths entirely away from the wall. Chromard finish fittings, made by **"Standard"**, are of finest quality, harmonize in design with the fixtures, are non-tarnishing, require no polishing and can be had to meet every installation and price requirement.

The Neo-Angle . . speed the bath—two at a time.

The Neo-Angle . . comfortably sit—soap and rub.

16

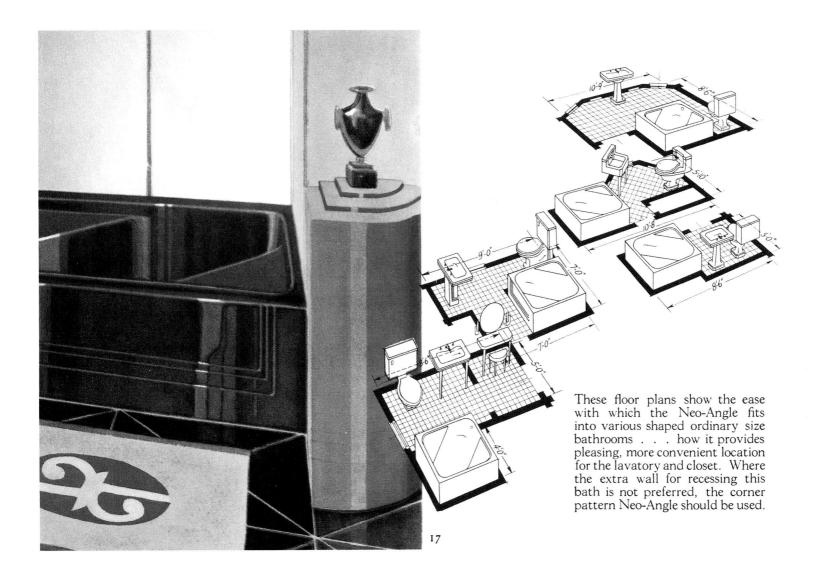

17

These floor plans show the ease with which the Neo-Angle fits into various shaped ordinary size bathrooms . . . how it provides pleasing, more convenient location for the lavatory and closet. Where the extra wall for recessing this bath is not preferred, the corner pattern Neo-Angle should be used.

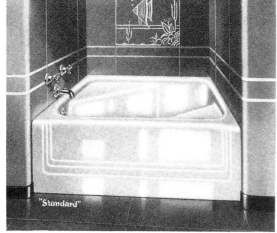

Neo-Angle - (Recess)

For the man who likes to take his shower with ample room to swing his arms or to sit down in perfect comfort and safety to wash his feet, the Neo-Angle should be his unhesitating choice. The mother who sees the new convenience of the comfortable seat when washing the children, even two at a time, in this ample bath, heartily approves his choice. And what a relief to grandmother who always had a little fear of the previous type tub.

With the convenience of its 2-inch lower height, the depth of water in the Neo-Angle is the same as in all other baths. It is 5 inches wider at the bottom and has the length of a 5½ foot built-in type of tub along the bottom, thus providing a greater bottom area for more comfortable immersion bathing and allowing plenty of room for standing under the shower spray. Where a 4 foot deep recess cannot be had, the corner Neo-Angle

Adapto - P 2454 N

has been made available. It has all the features of the recess pattern, can be fitted with shower rod and curtains, with fittings and outlets for right or left side as required.

Many persons will find in the long popular Pembroke, the bath that meets their requirements. It, like all "Standard" built-in baths, is available

Neo-Angle - (Corner)

Woodmere - P 2382 N

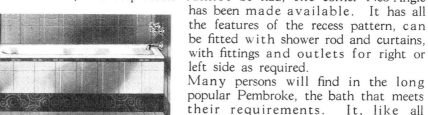

Essex (on Feet) - P 2500 D

18

in many styles of supply and drain fittings, with or without Shower, and with fittings on either end. The Woodmere is a wider, more massive bath of the Pembroke type. It can also be had in recess pattern and with fittings on either end.

The Adapto Bath lends itself to any decorative scheme, the one here being carried out with the same tile design in the front panel as in the walls.

The Essex is a quality bath for a restricted budget, or for use where a built-in bath is not practical. It is available on legs or on base as shown. The latter is preferable as having some of the advantages of the built-in type. The Knickerbocker, similar to the Essex in design except with a narrow rim, is for saving of space in small rooms.

Your Master Plumber can give you installed prices for any *"Standard"* Bath.

SIZES:—*Neo-Angle,* corner or recess; 49 x 50", (corner pattern, corner of wall to extreme front, 62"). *Woodmere,* corner or recess; 63 x 34", 69 x 34". *Pembroke,* corner; length, 55", 61", 67", 73"; width, 31". *Pembroke,* recess; length, 53", 59", 65", 71"; width, 31". *Recona,* length, 54", 60", 66"; width, 29". *Conred (like Recona, except for Corner);* length, 55", 61", 67"; width 29". *Adapto,* (can be installed four ways—recess, corner, pier, free standing); length, 55", 61", 67", 73"; width, 31". *Essex* on feet or base; length, 48", 54", 60", 66", 72"; width, 30". *Knickerbocker* on feet; length, 48", on feet or base 54", 60", 66"; width 26".

Pembroke - P 2305 J

Pembroke - P 2315 B

Essex (on Base) - P 2501 D

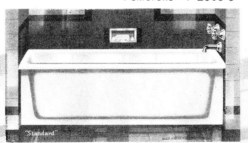

Recona - P 2480 N

Pembroke - P 2307 N

19

A Vigor Renewing Shower Must Be Included

Don't make the mistake of overlooking a shower—a mistake that many have regretted. After the walls are finished and decorated, they then realize how essential a shower is to their comfort. Its varied uses as a warm cleansing shower, a quick bath and rinse or as a cool refreshing, revivifying tonic shower, make it a fixture extremely desirable.

"Standard" Showers are available in many styles. Shown here are a few of the types—one with body sprays on each wall for installation in a recess and with a plate glass door, K 111 X; one with body sprays on one wall only, and for shower curtain, K 114 Y; one with a mixing valve, supplying hot, cold or tempered water by the turn of the handle, K 151 Y; one with two valves supplying the shower head, K 200 Y.

We suggest you see your Master Plumber who can show you many others as well as the complete line of bath, kitchen and laundry fixtures in the complete *"Standard"* Plumbing Fixture catalogue.

The K 661 "Annex-a" Shower is particularly attractive as a modernization fixture. It is easy to install and provides inexpensively a practical shower for baths already installed. Water is automatically directed to tub when valves are opened and cannot reach shower until the trip lever is operated. Turning the lever transfers water to shower and permits testing with hand before entering tub. Surprise showers are avoided.

20

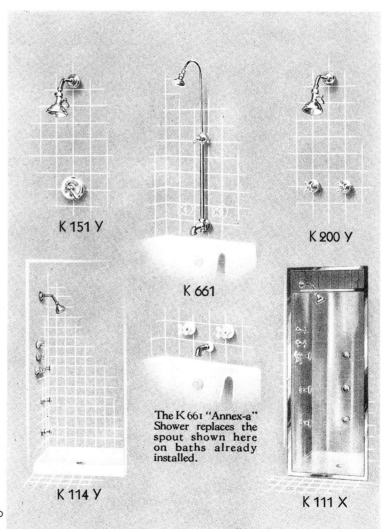

K 151 Y

K 200 Y

K 661

The K 661 "Annex-a" Shower replaces the spout shown here on baths already installed.

K 114 Y

K 111 X

The Most Important Feature of Home Sanitation

The importance of plumbing fixtures to daily living must give the water-closet the primary consideration. It is the one mechanical fixture requiring expert designing for steady, dependable, quick operation. The tank fittings must work properly for long periods without attention, completely immersed in water. The complete fixture must be sanitary and easily cleaned. You can readily see why water-closets should not be bought on price alone. There is only one safe procedure and that is to buy the best your budget permits from the various designs offered by a reputable manufacturer.

Efficiency and beauty of appearance—the essentials of good designing, have always been the guide marks to *"Standard"* improvements. This has resulted in one-piece construction—in lavatories, baths, sinks—but for many years not achieved in water-closets.

Now the *"Standard"* One-Piece Closet design, developed within the past few years, with the greatest selling record of all *"Standard"* closets in the short time after its introduction, proves that it embodies what home owners want—a closet so quiet it cannot be heard outside the room—so compact that it can be placed under windows or cupboards—so attractive as to harmonize with the finest bathroom decorative scheme—and self-supporting so that it can be placed anywhere. Here is the ideal closet for any bathroom, large or small.

Shown on this page is the very latest in closet design—the Master One-Piece, F 2148 A. Beautifully proportioned, yet compact, with elongated rim (a superior sanitary feature), with improved flushing mechanism to assure the quietest positive flush, it represents the very finest closet that can be installed.

21

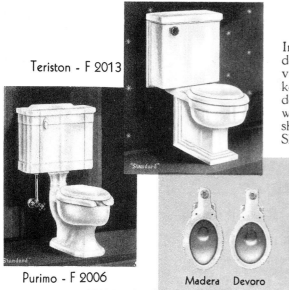

Teriston - F 2013

Purimo - F 2006

Madera   Devoro

In selecting a **"Standard"** Water-closet, you can safely let your budget and design preference be your guide. All **"Standard"** Closets are made of genuine vitreous china, the ideal material. It is hard, non-absorbent, easy to clean and keeps its beauty of surface indefinitely. Closets have **"Standard"** brass fittings designed to provide dependable mechanical operation. The closets are supplied with "Church" brand seats, of well-seasoned wood with non-absorbent, easy to clean sheet covering, in white or in color, plain or sea-pearl to match the fixture . . . Shown on these pages are closets widely used in home installation. The principal bowl differences are shown at the left. The elongated design is achieving preference everywhere as it provides surer sanitary features. The round front bowl is more economical in price and is often used where space is a factor . . . The Master One-Piece, shown on page 21 and the One-Piece, F 2149 A (with round front bowl) shown in color on page 23 and in bathrooms throughout this book, are rapidly becoming the most preferred closets for distinctive bathrooms . . . The Teriston syphon-jet closet has a modern straight line treatment matching the Neo-Classic lines of lavatories and baths. The unit appearance of the Teriston with its elimination of narrow flush connection is also obtainable in a more economical closet,

Master Devoro - F 2036

Madera - F 2103

Siacto - F 2145

Modernus - F 2186

22

the Moderno, F 2197, illustrated on Page 6 . . . The Purimo has a large bowl with extended front and cut-out back, thus assuring minimum of soiling space. The Madera with elongated bowl, and Devoro with regular round front bowl, are widely used syphon-jet closets. The Master Madera and Master Devoro have an advanced design tank with high quality hushed type fittings . . . The Siacto Closet is a dependable sanitary closet of the syphon action type and is offered at a moderate price. The Modernus is a washdown type closet, with the straight front design. It meets fully the demand for strictest economy . . . "Standard" Compact is a modern design closet at a low cost and having unusual space and water saving features. Like the "Standard" One-Piece it meets the trend toward free from the wall closets making it ideal for remodeling.

SIZES: Width over-all and back to front:

Master One-Piece, 23 x 28"; One-Piece, 22 x 26½"; *Purimo, Madera*, 23 x 30"; *Teriston*, 21 x 30"; *Master Devoro*, 23 x 28"; *Siacto*, 21 x 28"; *Modernus, Moderno and Compact*, 21 x 27".

A Most Appreciated
Additional Convenience

In every home the morning rush to work and school or the evening preparation for visiting, entertainment, etc., puts excessive demands upon the bathroom. If you have guests, the lack of sufficient toilet rooms may be embarrassing. Why not avoid all this by having a small convenient room partitioned off the hall or converted from an unused closet? There need be no embarrassment if the Quiet "Standard" One-Piece Closet, shown in room at right, is used.

Compact - F 2140

23

The Kitchen Advances.

The acknowledged center of the Kitchen is the sink. The entire room should be built around it. **"Standard"** has pioneered in sink advances, giving to grateful housewives the one-piece sink, the yard-stick-high sink, the eight inch deep and eight inch back sink, the Electric Dishwasher.

Here is the newest **"Standard"** achievement—the Neo-Line. Graceful curves give beauty of design, oval sink compartment accommodates today's dishpan models and is easier to clean, the large double strainer with liftout crumb cup is more convenient; non-tarnishing Chromard fittings are up out of the way, and the integral shelf has a dozen uses that add efficiency and save kitchen labor. The Neo-Line is furnished either with a 6" apron or a roll-rim. An attractive steel cabinet can be had with the roll-rim type—42" with sink on left, P 6648, sink on right, P 6649, 60" double drain-board, P 6651. This sink is just being introduced and is meeting with instant favor.

For a really distinctive kitchen you will want a Neo-Line.

Apron Type
P 6646, Sink on left; P 6647, Sink on right; size 42 x 22". P 6650, double drain-board; 60 x 22". Width of Shelf, 6". Height of Back, 8", Depth of Sink, 6", Apron 6".

Roll-Rim Type
(less cabinets)
42" Sink on left, P 6652, Sink on right, P 6653, 60" double drain-board, P 6654.

Neo-Line - P 6646

Neo-Line - P 6650

24

110

A Cabinet For Efficiency

Most homes built within the past few years have included step-saving, time-saving cabinets as part of the kitchen construction. These may be in a corner or along an entire wall; they are of attractively finished wood or metal.

Homes with pantries or other storage spaces may not need an installation of cabinets in the kitchen; old homes may not have space for them. But every home can well use and easily afford the new Sinkabnets, illustrated.

These Sinkabnets consist of regular type sinks with all-steel cabinets set underneath and provide storage spaces so long needed for the dishpan, dishmop, pot cleaners, lids, soaps, knives, etc., used constantly around the kitchen.

Two designs of regular "Standard" Sinks are illustrated with metal cabinets. The single drain-board type can also be had without cabinets—P 6815 with left sink, P 6816 with right sink, are 20 inches wide. The double drain-board Hudson, less cabinet in 22 inch width is P 6814. The Norton, less cabinet, is P 6840, and is 60, 72 and 84 inches long.

Those owners who prefer a larger double drain-board sink or whose budget permits a more substantial item will be interested in the Norton sink.

This sink is 25 inches wide and can be had with plain ends as shown, a splash back at either right or left end or at both ends. The types with splash backs allow cabinets not only underneath but at left or right.

25

Norton - P 6850 QS

Warren - P 6818 E

Warren with Left Drain-board
P 6819 E

Sizes: P 6818, P 6819
42 x 20", 52 x 20".

The 52" size has 2 drawers and small cupboard on the side under drain-board.

Hudson—P 6817 QS, same as P 6818, except with two drain-boards, and with swinging spout faucet; drawers and cupboard under each drain-board.
Size: 60 x 22".

Norton—P 6850 QS
Sizes:
60 x 25", 72 x 25"

As one kitchen efficiency expert says in regard to present kitchen designing, "Kitchens are not only beautiful and comfortable, but so arranged that they have become the production department of the home, the business office and the social center, all rolled into one."

The Sink is the work center of the kitchen and is entitled to the place under the window for light, air and restful view. Why? Because so much of the preparatory work is at the sink. With this in mind "Standard" originated the Three 8's sink for placing under low windows. The 8" low back, since adopted universally as the extreme height for all kitchen sinks, permitted the elevation of the rim of sink to yard-stick high.

The time-tested worth of "Standard" Sinks made of glistening enamel on rigid cast iron is known to the millions of home owners who have had them in their kitchens for many years. The Schenley is really a very de luxe design intended for the kitchen of distinctive arrangement and decorative scheme. The owner who prefers the Neo-Classic motif in his bathroom fixtures will appreciate this same design in the sink, for his kitchen will doubtless be as well planned as his bathroom. Illustrated also are three models of the Three 8's. The same designs are available with 6-inch deep sink.

Although the first cost of sinks made of Acid-Resisting Enamel is slightly higher, the replacement expense it eliminates and the longer life and beauty it gives to the fixtures, result in an appreciable saving. All enameled "Standard" Sinks can be obtained in Acid-Resisting Enamel.

Write for circular on choosing the right sink for your kitchen. It contains additional illustrations of sinks and cabinets.

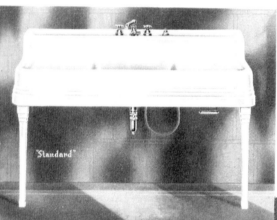

Schenley - P 6645

The Schenley has a 6-inch back, 8-inch deep front, 8-inch deep sink, with a broad shelf containing the fittings, as in the Neo-Line. There is a rubber hose and spray through the shelf also. A Chromard utensil drawer, which swings down when in use, and up and out of the way when not needed, can be had if desired. Size of Sink: Length overall 62 inches, width 27 inches.

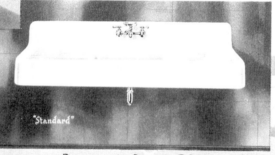

Brentwood - P 6660 QS

26

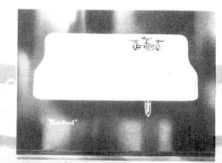

Glenmere - P 6657 QS

Many more types of time-tested enameled cast-iron sinks are available. See your Master Plumber's General Catalogue. He will be glad to quote installed price on any size or design.

While regularly furnished with grid type strainer, most "Standard" Sinks can be furnished with K 878 double strainer at slight extra cost. It permits the sink compartment to be used as a dishpan and provides additional safeguard against clogging the waste lines. Food particles lodge in the cup strainer and when the cup is lifted the water drains off.

SIZES: *Brentwood* (Three 8's); P 6660 Q S, 60 x 22", 74 x 22", 78 x 22", *Clinton* (6" Sink); P 6710 Q S, 60 x 22", 74 x 20", 78 x 22". *Glenmere* (Three 8's); P 6657 Q S, P 6656 Q S (left sink), 42 x 22", 52 x 22", *Bedford* (6" Sink); P 6707 Q S, P 6706 Q S (left Sink), 42 x 20", 52 x 20", 60 x 22". *Stratford* (Three 8's); P 6665 Q S, P 6666 Q S (right corner), 52 x 22", *Concord* (6" Sink); P 6715 Q S, P 6716 Q S (right corner), 42 x 20", 52 x 20", 60 x 22".

The Radcliff, P 7432 Q S, (P 7433 Q S with sink on right) is a sink and laundry tray combination, ideal for apartments, small kitchens, or homes with no laundry facilities. The 13-inch deep tray is ideal for the washing of linens, silks and light articles of clothing. The sink compartment is 8 inches deep, back is 8 inches high. The tray cover is reversible allowing use as a sink or a laundry tray. This fixture is made in three sizes, 36 x 22", 43 x 22", and 51 x 24".

Enameled cast-iron is the best material for laundry trays. It is impervious to dirt and grease, is easy to clean, and brightens the laundry. Your Master Plumber can show you a number of enameled trays in his General Catalogue. The Montrose, here shown, is the most economical of a variety of "Standard" trays, costing very little more than trays of other materials. It is 48 x 23 inches over all.

K 878

Stratford - P 6665 QS

Montrose - P 7381 B

Radcliff - P 7432 QS

27

Save Labor, Save Time, Save Hands

Most housewives face the one remaining kitchen drudgery, that of washing dishes three times a day, year in and out, without a murmur, merely from force of habit or from resignation to the situation. But do you call it good planning to thoughtlessly permit this unending task (more than 12 hours a week in the average family) in order to save the slight difference between the cost of a **"Standard"** Electric Dishwasher and Sink and the sink without this feature?

The **"Standard"** Dishwasher, one of the earliest in the home field, is sturdily constructed, has simple trouble-free mechanism, is efficient, economical and easy to operate. Strong sprays of water (too hot for the hands) play upon every surface of every dish or piece of silverware, revolving from the force of the water action in a sturdy basket. It is not necessary to dry the dishes with a towel but even if one prefers to do so the drying is much quicker and easier.

Save these back-breaking sessions at the sink, save 12 hours of weekly labor, avoid reddened hands. And dishes, due to the scalding water (but little more is used than in hand washing) are beyond question more sanitary and are without a trace of grease or soap. The amount of electricity used in a whole month won't cost as much as a pound of butter. The dishwasher, which can be installed separately or built-in with adjacent drainboards, work-tops or cabinets, has a generous size sink compartment on the right. Write for circular giving complete information and mechanical details.

A dishwasher should be in every modern home. This simple, trouble-free **"Standard"** Dishwasher, at a cost no greater than a better type sink, answers the demand for this most needed home convenience.

"Standard" Electric Dishwasher - P 6910

28

"Standard" Leads in Design and Material Developments

"Standard" the largest manufacturer of plumbing fixtures, with nearly a half century of experience, has always led in advances in their construction and styling and, more than any one agency, has brought the bathroom from one of mere utilitarian purpose to the most interesting room in the home. In addition to the Neo-Classic, Neo-Angle, Neo-Line and Mastercraft designs, unit construction, (as particularly exemplified in the One-Piece Closet), and correctly derived colors, "Standard" has introduced outstandingly more beautiful and durable finishes. Acid-Resisting Enamel and Chromard were developed by "Standard". Fruit and vegetable acids do not roughen or discolor plumbing fixtures made of Acid-Resisting Enamel. Not even the cleaning acids used by the tile setters can mar its smooth, glossy surface. It is easy to clean and to keep clean. With a minimum of care it stays spotless and bright. It costs slightly more than regular enamel, but the longer life and beauty it gives the fixtures, result in an appreciable saving. It is identified by the trade-mark "Standard" A-R.

Chromard is the application of chromium plating to brass fittings that is rapidly supplanting nickel-plate as it has a more beautiful color, which is akin to silver, and does not tarnish. Unlike silver or nickel it requires no polishing; you merely use soap and a damp cloth to clean.

Your Protection Is In The Name, "Standard"

"Standard" This trade-mark is printed permanently under the glaze of Vitreous China plumbing fixtures, printed permanently in the enamel of plumbing fixtures made of regular enamel, and cast or stamped in the metal of brass fittings.

RE-NU This word on "Standard" Brass Goods indicates renewable seats and threads, a "Standard" feature.

"Standard"-A-R This trade-mark, printed permanently in the enamel, identifies plumbing fixtures made of "Standard" Acid-Resisting Enamel.

Church Seats "Church" brand Seats, which are regular equipment on "Standard" water-closets, are identified by this trade-mark, which is pressed into the under side of the seat.

And look for the green label affixed to all enameled fixtures, which also identifies them as "Standard" and which gives you an added safeguard, with its warning to all who handle or work around the fixture at the time of installation to "be careful". This further assures you of having a satisfactory fixture in all its original, sparkling beauty.

29

Chromard is the Trend in Sink and Bathroom Fittings

The beauty and easy cleaning of Chromard Finish and the fact that it will not tarnish, has had much to do with the tremendous favor of all-metal fittings. The graceful lines and greater beauty of design possible in metal, has had its part in this new mode.

But while you find all this in the finish of *"Standard"* Bath, Sink and Lavatory Fittings, remember that they are just as honest in the basic metal and in sturdy, mechanically correct construction. It is easy to make inferior brass look beautiful. The word *"Standard"* stamped or cast in the metal assures you that you are getting dependable fixtures with quality under the glistening surface, that will give long satisfactory use. The word **RE-NU** adds to that service as it indicates a fitting in which it is possible to renew worn parts at slight expense.

Shown on this page are illustrations of sink faucets of regular design, K 902 SY and the superior heavy cast brass Mastercraft pattern with valves concealed behind the sink back, K 882 SY. Shown also is a faucet with hose and spray, K 907 SY. Single lavatory faucets can be had in several types, with lever or 4-arm handles. Two styles each of combination bath fittings, K 325 Y and K 610 Y, and of combination lavatory fittings, K 780 Y and K 701 Y, supplying water through a single spout and the exquisitely patterned Mastercraft heavy cast brass lavatory fitting, K 701 X, are shown.

"Standard" is the world's largest producer of Plumbers Brass Goods. *"Standard"* fittings *fit* *"Standard"* fixtures.

30

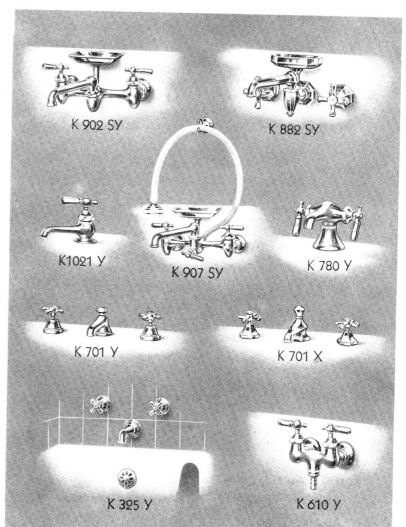

K 902 SY

K 882 SY

K1021 Y

K 907 SY

K 780 Y

K 701 Y

K 701 X

K 325 Y

K 610 Y

How To Get What You Want In "Standard" Plumbing Fixtures

Visit a Showroom displaying "Standard" fixtures. There you can see many actual fixtures, discuss your problems, secure help in originating color schemes and in developing pleasing bathroom arrangements. Specifications providing for their installation will be written for you without charge.

If you cannot visit a "Standard" or Wholesaler's Showroom, make your selection from this book, then take the book to your Plumber and in it point out the fixtures and fittings you want. If this book does not illustrate what you have in mind, you are sure to find it in his General Catalogue.

Consult Your Master Plumber

Your Master Plumber is your neighbor. He is interested in your Plumbing problems, he knows how best to meet them, he will give you a quality installation conforming to all local plumbing requirements, at the lowest possible prices. Consult with him regarding which "Standard" plumbing fixtures and fittings are best for your particular needs.

"Standard" Showrooms, Branches and Sales Offices

For full information about "Standard" Fixtures, see your Master Plumber or write or call at any "Standard" Unit listed below:

AKRON, O.	COLUMBUS, O.	HUNTINGTON, W. VA.	MONTGOMERY, ALA.	SAN ANTONIO, TEXAS
ALTOONA, PA.	DALLAS, TEXAS	JOLIET, ILL.	NASHVILLE, TENN.	SAN FRANCISCO, CALIF.
ATLANTA, GA.	DENVER, COLO.	KANSAS CITY, MO.	NEWARK, N. J.	SEATTLE, WASH.
BALTIMORE, MD.	DETROIT, MICH.	KNOXVILLE, TENN.	NEW ORLEANS, LA.	SHREVEPORT, LA.
BEAUMONT, TEXAS	EAST ST. LOUIS, ILL.	LAS VEGAS, NEV.	NEW YORK, N. Y.	SOUTH BEND, IND.
BIRMINGHAM, ALA.	EL PASO, TEXAS	LONG ISLAND CITY, N. Y.	PEORIA, ILL.	SPRINGFIELD, MASS.
BOSTON, MASS.	ERIE, PA.	LOS ANGELES, CALIF.	PHILADELPHIA, PA.	SYRACUSE, N. Y.
BUFFALO, N. Y.	EVANSVILLE, IND.	LOUISVILLE, KY.	PHOENIX, ARIZ.	TOLEDO, O.
CANTON, O.	FORT WAYNE, IND.	MANSFIELD, O.	PITTSBURGH, PA.	TUCSON, ARIZ.
CHICAGO, ILL.	FORT WORTH, TEXAS	MEMPHIS, TENN.	PORTLAND, ORE.	TYLER, TEXAS
CINCINNATI, O.	GRAND RAPIDS, MICH.	MILWAUKEE, WIS.	ROCK ISLAND, ILL.	WASHINGTON, D. C.
CLEVELAND, O.	HOUSTON, TEXAS	MINNEAPOLIS, MINN.	ST. LOUIS, MO.	WHEELING, W. VA.

Standard Sanitary Mfg. Co.

General Offices, Pittsburgh, Pa.

Division of AMERICAN RADIATOR & STANDARD SANITARY CORPORATION

31

COLOR BRINGS A REFRESHING
NEW BEAUTY TO THE BATHROOM

Color in plumbing fixtures has steadily increased in popularity since its introduction a few years ago. The all-white bathroom is no longer favored as the perfect ideal of sanitation. Even with white fixtures, color is used freely in the decorative scheme.

Every one loves color, though some hesitate to make use of color freely. They feel that they will tire of the same color fixtures after a while. But do they tire of their furniture and buy new each year? No! They may not replace the tapestry upholstering, but they depend on new wall and floor coverings, new drapes, etc., for a complete and satisfying change.

This is just as logical with "Standard" Fixtures in color, because "Standard" Fixture Colors were selected by an artist of international standing. Each color had to be beautiful, it had to compliment the skin but primarily it had to be a proper basic or key color for correct and livable bathroom color schemes.

Of the wide choice of ten "Standard" colors, listed on the opposite page, you select your favorite one, then with "Standard" literature offering helpful suggestions, supplementing your own good taste, you can hardly fail to obtain a pleasing result, much more so than any all-one-color bathroom could possibly be.

Harmony or pleasing contrast are both effective, but in no case should a wall color be chosen that matches the color of the fixtures. Rooms with northern exposures should have warm color schemes, those with southern exposures, cool schemes. This thought relates principally to the fixtures, as "Standard" fixture colors were derived to be used as base or key colors for bathroom decorative schemes.

If you have an unusual bathroom in arrangement or decoration in prospect and are not quite sure how to approach the color angle, write the nearest "Standard" unit, and they will consult with our color and decoration experts regarding your problem.

Whenever you desire a change, you can select from a dozen different combinations of color in wall coverings, floor coverings, draperies, shower curtains and woodwork that can be changed at minimum expense without requiring a change of fixture color or fittings, so that with the fixtures still in your same favorite color as before, the bathroom as a whole unit will be entirely different, new and smart. Color costs so little more than white and this additional cost is only on the bare fixtures not on the fittings. The installation cost is no higher. Let us, finally, repeat our initial suggestion—plan wisely, choose well, choose "Standard" —and you are sure to have a bathroom and kitchen that will add beauty to your home comfort and convenience to your family, value to your investment and satisfaction to your guests, your friends, and yourself for many years to come.

32

"Standard" Plumbing Fixture Colors

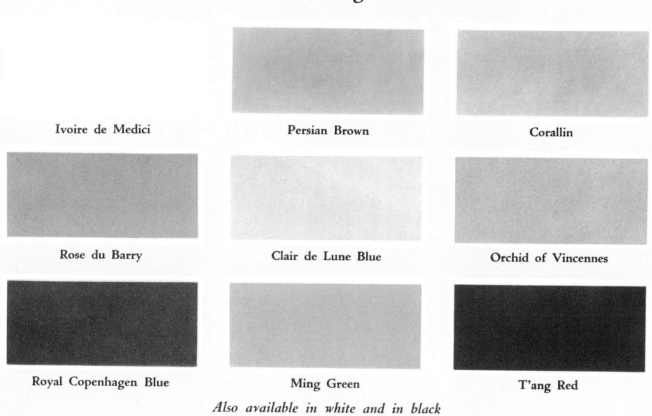

Ivoire de Medici	Persian Brown	Corallin
Rose du Barry	Clair de Lune Blue	Orchid of Vincennes
Royal Copenhagen Blue	Ming Green	T'ang Red

Also available in white and in black

Bathroom Fixture Sources

The companies listed here provide a variety of antique, reproduction and new bathroom fixtures that may be appropriate for your period bathroom. Items and services include sinks and tubs, toilets and seats, accessories (towel racks, soap dishes and similar items), salvaged fixtures, refinishing services and custom manufacturing. Most companies sell by mail order; some also (or only) have retail outlets that you may visit; a few sell only through distributors, designers or architects. If you have or are trying to recreate an early 20th-century bathroom similar to those presented here, providing suppliers with a photograph or drawing or a photocopy of items in this book may help ensure suitable fixtures.

These listings were derived primarily from *The Old-House Journal Catalog,* compiled by *The Old-House Journal* (© 1988 by Old-House Journal Corp.), 935 Ninth Street, Brooklyn, N.Y. 11215 (718) 636-4514. Some listings are from *The Sixth Old House Catalogue* compiled by Lawrence Grow (© 1988 by The Main Street Press), William Case House, Pittstown, N.J. 08867 (201) 735-9424. Both books are excellent sources for thousands of items and services useful in rehabilitating old houses and other buildings, including more information on the companies here. Additionally, they include listings of tile suitable for bathrooms, a subject covered also in *Floor Coverings for Historic Buildings,* by Helene Von Rosenstiel and Gail Caskey Winkler (1988, The Preservation Press), 1785 Massachusetts Avenue, N.W., Washington, D.C. 20036 (202) 673-4058.

A-Ball Plumbing Supply
1703 West Burnside Street
Portland, Ore. 97209
(503) 228-0026

American Standard
U.S. Plumbing Products
One Centennial Plaza
Piscataway, N.J. 08855
(201) 980-3000

Antique Baths and Kitchens
2220 Carlton Way
Santa Barbara, Calif. 93109
(805) 962-8598

Antique Hardware Store
43 Bridge Street
Frenchtown, N.J. 08825
(800) 422-9982
(201) 996-4040

Baldwin Hardware Corporation
841 Wyomissing Boulevard
Box 15048
Reading, Pa. 19612
(215) 777-7811

Bathlines
2154 North Halsted Street
Chicago, Ill. 60614
(312) 472-0777

Bathmasters International
1595 Miller Road
Imperial, Mo. 63052
(314) 464-3242

Besco Plumbing and Heating Sales
729 Atlantic Avenue
Boston, Mass. 02111
(617) 423-4535

The Broadway Collection
250 North Troost
Olathe, Kans. 66061
(800) 843-3962

Cheviot Products
Box F110-35
Blaine, Wash. 98230
(604) 420-8989

Chicago Faucet Company
2100 South Nuclear Drive
Des Plaines, Ill. 60018
(312) 694-4400

Consumer Supply Company
1110 West Lake
Chicago, Ill. 60607
(312) 666-6080

Crawford's Old House Store
550 Elizabeth Street
Waukesha, Wis. 53186
(414) 542-0685

D.E.A./Bathroom Machineries
495 Main Street
Box 1020
Murphys, Calif. 95247
(209) 728-2031

Decorative Hardware Studio
P.O. Box 627
180 Hunts Lane
Chappaqua, N.Y. 10514
(914) 238-5251

Decorum
235-237 Commercial Street
Portland, Maine 04101
(207) 775-3346

Dentro Plumbing Specialties
63-16 Woodhaven Boulevard
Rego Park, N.Y. 11374
(718) 672-6882

DeWeese Woodworking
Highway 492
P.O. Box 576
Philadelphia, Miss. 39350
(601) 656-4951

DuraGlaze Service
1114 Harpeth Industrial
Franklin, Tenn. 37064
(615) 790-8827

Eljer Plumbingware
P.O. Box 869037
Plano, Tex. 75086
(214) 881-7177

George Taylor Specialties Company
187 Lafayette Street
New York, N.Y. 10013
(212) 226-5369

Great American Salvage
34 Cooper Square
New York, N.Y. 10003
(212) 505-0070

Heads Up
133 Copeland Street
Petaluma, Calif. 94952
(800) 358-9080
(707) 762-5548

Hippo Hardware and Trading Company
201 S.E. 12th Avenue
Portland, Ore. 97214
(503) 231-1444

John Kruesel's General Merchandise
22 Third Street, S.W.
Rochester, Minn. 55902
(507) 289-8049

Kohler Company
Kohler, Wis. 53044
(414) 457-4441

Lenape Products
P.O. Box 117
Pennington Industrial Center
Pennington, N.J. 08534
(609) 737-0206

Lena's Antique Bathroom Fixtures
P.O. Box 1022
Bethel Island, Calif. 94511
(415) 625-4878

Luwa Corporation
Builder Products Division
P.O. Box 16348
Charlotte, N.C. 28297-6348
(704) 394-8341

Mac the Antique Plumber
885 57th Street
Sacramento, Calif. 95819
(916) 454-4507

Masterworks
8558 I Lee Highway
Fairfax, Va. 22031
(703) 849-8384

Off the Wall, Architectural Antiques
950 Glenneyre Street
Laguna Beach, Calif. 92651
(714) 497-4000

Old and Elegant Distributing
10203 Main Street Lane
Bellevue, Wash. 98004
(206) 455-4660

Old House Store
2154 North Halstead Street
Chicago, Ill. 60614
(312) 472-0777

Ole Fashion Things
402 S.W. Evangeline Thruway
Lafayette, La. 70501
(318) 234-7963

Perma Ceram Enterprises
65 Smithtown Boulevard
Smithtown, N.Y. 11787
(516) 724-1205

Remodelers and Renovators
Box 45478
Boise, Idaho 83704
(800) 456-2135
(208) 634-2412

Renovation Concepts
213 Washington Avenue, North
Minneapolis, Minn. 55401
(612) 333-5766

Restoration Works
810 Main Street
P.O. Box 486
Buffalo, N.Y. 14205
(716) 856-8000

Roy Electric Company
1054 Coney Island Avenue
Brooklyn, N.Y. 11230
(718) 339-6311

St. Thomas Creations
79-25 Denbrook Road
San Diego, Calif. 92126
(619) 530-1940

The Sink Factory
2140 San Pablo Avenue
Berkeley, Calif. 94702
(415) 540-8193

Steptoe's Old House Store
322 Geary Avenue
Toronto, Ontario, Canada M6H 2C7
(416) 537-5772

Sunrise Specialty Company
2204 San Pablo Avenue
Berkeley, Calif. 94702
(415) 845-4751

Vintage Plumbing Specialties
9645 Sylvia Avenue
Northridge, Calif. 91324
(818) 772-6353

**Vintage Tub and Sink
Restoration Service**
701 Center Street
Ludlow, Mass. 01056
(413) 589-0769

Watercolors
Garrison on Hudson, N.Y. 10524
(914) 424-3327

Further Reading

See also the notes to the Introduction.

Evers, Christopher. "The Circulatory and Excretory Systems: Water Supply and Waste Disposal." In *The Old-House Doctor.* Woodstock, N.Y.: Overlook Press, 1986.

J. L. Mott Iron Works. *Victorian Plumbing Fixtures for Bathrooms and Kitchens.* Catalog G, 1888. Mineola, N.Y.: Dover Publications, 1987.

Kira, Alexander. *The Bathroom.* New York: Viking Press, 1976.

Lambton, Lucinda. *Chambers of Delight.* London: Gordon Fraser Gallery, 1983.

_____ . *Temples of Convenience.* New York: St. Martin's Press, 1978.

Lindstrom, Bekka. "Post-Victorian Interiors: Bathrooms," *Old-House Journal,* November–December 1987, pp. 33–35.

Palmer, Roy. *The Water Closet: A New History.* North Pomfret, Vt.: David and Charles, 1973.

Reyburn, Wallace. *Flushed With Pride: The Story of Thomas Crapper.* Englewood Cliffs, N.J.: Prentice-Hall, 1970.

Reynolds, Reginald. *Cleanliness and Godliness: or, The Further Metamorphosis.* 1943. Reprint. New York: Harcourt Brace Jovanovich, 1976.

Rudolfsky, Bernard. "Uncleanliness and Ungodliness: A Rapid Survey of Bathing Costumes and Bathroom History," *Interior Design,* June 1984, pp. 212–21.

Winkler, Gail Caskey, and Roger W. Moss. "How the Bathroom Got White Tiles. . .and Other Victorian Tales," *Historic Preservation,* February 1984, pp. 33–35.

Wright, Lawrence. *Clean and Decent: The Fascinating History of the Bathroom and the Water Closet.* 1960. Reprint. Boston: Routledge and Kegan Paul, 1984.

Authors

GAIL CASKEY WINKLER, Ph.D., ASID, is the senior partner of LCA Associates, Philadelphia, which provides design and restoration services to museums, corporations, organizations and individuals. She is coauthor with Roger W. Moss of *Victorian Interior Decoration* and *Victorian Exterior Decoration* (1986, 1987, Henry Holt) and with Helene Von Rosenstiel of *Floor Coverings for Historic Buildings* (1988, The Preservation Press), winner of the annual publications prize awarded by the American Society of Interior Designers Educational Foundation. She is at work on *The Victorian Woman's Home: Godey's Lady's Book and the American Home 1830–1877,* to be published by Henry Holt. She lectures throughout the United States and teaches in the Historic Preservation Program, Graduate School of Fine Arts, University of Pennsylvania.

CHARLES E. FISHER III of Greenbelt, Md., has more than 15 years' experience with the historic preservation programs of the National Park Service in Washington, D.C. He is editor of the National Park Service's Preservation Tech Notes Series and has edited and written portions of *The Interiors Handbook for Historic Buildings, The Window Handbook: Successful Strategies for Rehabilitating Windows in Historic Buildings* and *The Window Workbook for Historic Buildings.* Fisher has written numerous articles on historic preservation technology and is actively involved in lecturing and planning technical workshops and conferences on the rehabilitation of historic buildings, such as the 1988 Interiors Conference and Exposition for Historic Buildings.

Other Preservation Press Books

REHABILITATION

Respectful Rehabilitation: Answers to Your Questions About Old Buildings
National Park Service. A "Dear Abby" for old buildings that answers 150 of the most-asked questions about rehabilitating old houses and other historic buildings. 200 pp., illus., biblio., index. Order no. 10048. $12.95 pb.

Masonry: How to Care for Old and Historic Brick and Stone
Mark London. Explains how to understand and treat masonry problems from foundations to roofs and maintain and repair buildings from cleaning and repointing to solving moisture problems. 208 pp., illus., biblio., index. Order no. 10061. $12.95 pb.

New Life for Old Houses
George Stephen. A down-to-earth guide to all the design and rehabilitation decisions homeowners face in properly restoring their old houses. 272 pp., illus., biblio., append., index. Order no. 10141. $12.95 pb.

INTERIORS

Fabrics for Historic Buildings
Jane C. Nylander. 3rd edition. A popular primer that gives practical advice on selecting and using reproductions of historic fabrics. Includes an illustrated catalog of 550 reproduction fabrics and a list of manufacturers. 160 pp., illus., gloss., biblio. Order no. 10020. $13.95 pb.

Floor Coverings for Historic Buildings
Helene Von Rosenstiel and Gail Caskey Winkler. Presents historical overviews of authentic period reproduction floor coverings from wood floors and linoleum to hooked and woven rugs. Also provides purchasing information for 475 patterns available today. 284 pp., illus., gloss., biblio. Order no. 10057. $14.95 pb.

Lighting for Historic Buildings
Roger W. Moss. Describes the history of lighting from the colonial era through the 1920s and arranges several hundred reproduction fixtures by original energy source (candle, gas, gas-electric and electric) and type (chandeliers, sconces and lanterns). 192 pp., illus., gloss., biblio. Order no. 10072. $13.95 pb.

Wallpapers for Historic Buildings
Richard C. Nylander. Shows how to select authentic reproductions of historic wallpapers and where to buy more than 350 recommended patterns. 128 pp., illus., gloss., biblio. Order no. 10050. $13.95 pb.

To request a complete list of Preservation Press books, please see the accompanying order form.

ORDER FORM

THE PRESERVATION PRESS
National Trust for Historic Preservation
1785 Massachusetts Avenue, N.W.
Washington, D.C. 20036

To order by telephone, call the National Trust
Mail-Order Division at (202) 673-4200.

Name

Address

City   State   Zip

Telephone

Quantity   Title

Ship as a gift to

Name

Address

City   State   Zip

Order no.   Price   Total

☐ Please send complete publications list.

☐ Check (payable to National Trust) enclosed

☐ VISA   ☐ MasterCard   ☐ AmExpress

Account no.

Expiration date   Day telephone

Signature

*Residents of Calif., Colo., D.C., Ill., Iowa, La., Md.,
Mass., N.Y., Pa., S.C., Tex. and Va. add applicable
sales tax.

SUBTOTAL $ _____

Less 10% Trust members' discount $ _____

Sales tax where applicable* $ _____

Shipping and handling (see below) $ _____

Individual ($15) or Family ($20)

Trust membership $ _____

TOTAL $ _____

Shipping and handling: 1-2 books, $3; 3-5 books,
$5; 6+ books, $8; outside the U.S., $3 per book.
Please allow a minimum of three weeks for delivery.